Whether you have been our neighbors or our friends & family separated by hundreds of miles, you have helped us arrive to this moment. Each photo is a story, a moment, and you have shared in them with us.

To those people, we dedicate this book and these experiences.

Winter

"Winter is the time for comfort, for good food and warmth, for the touch of a friendly hand and for a talk beside the fire: it is the time for home."

– Edith Sitwell

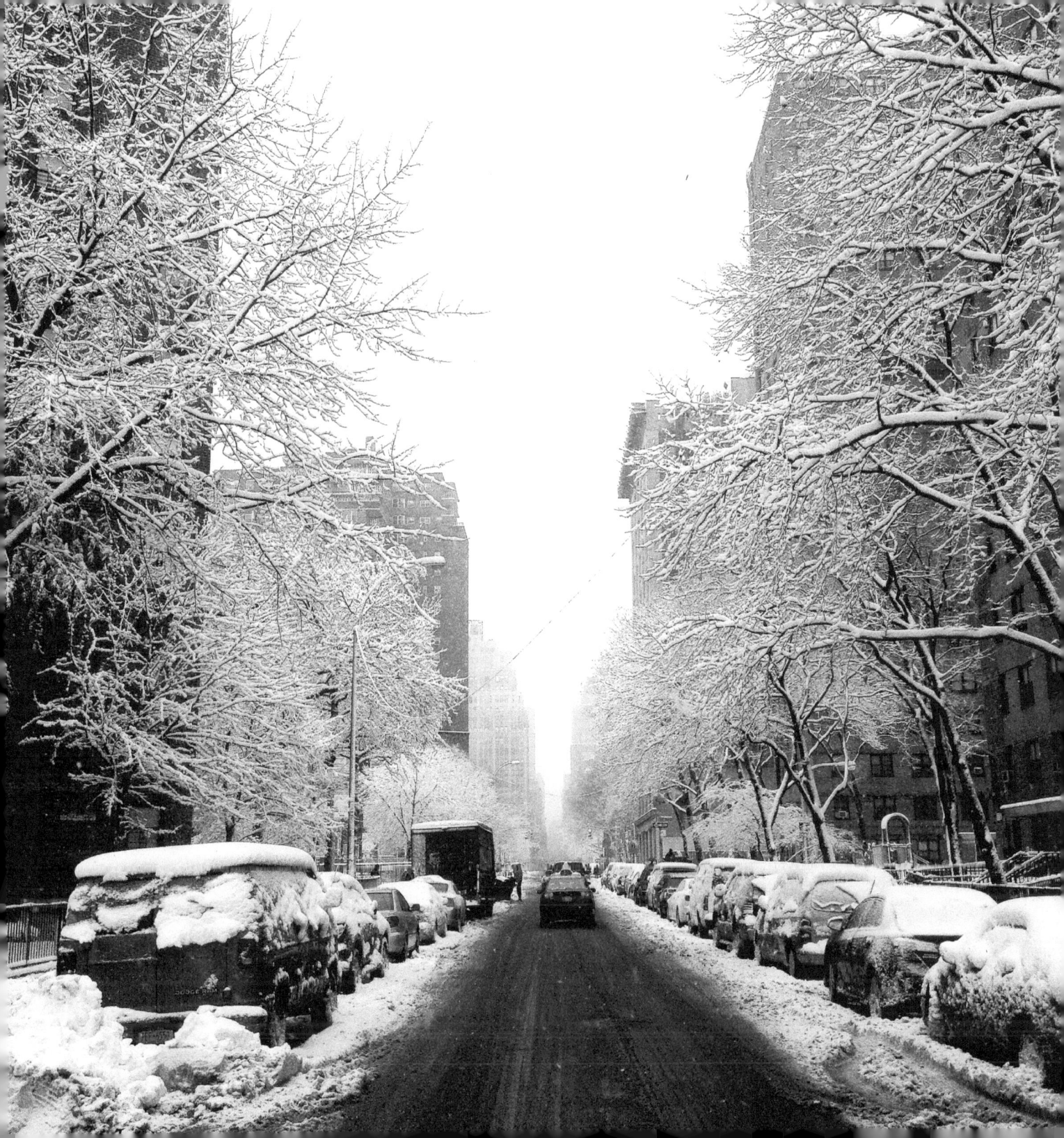

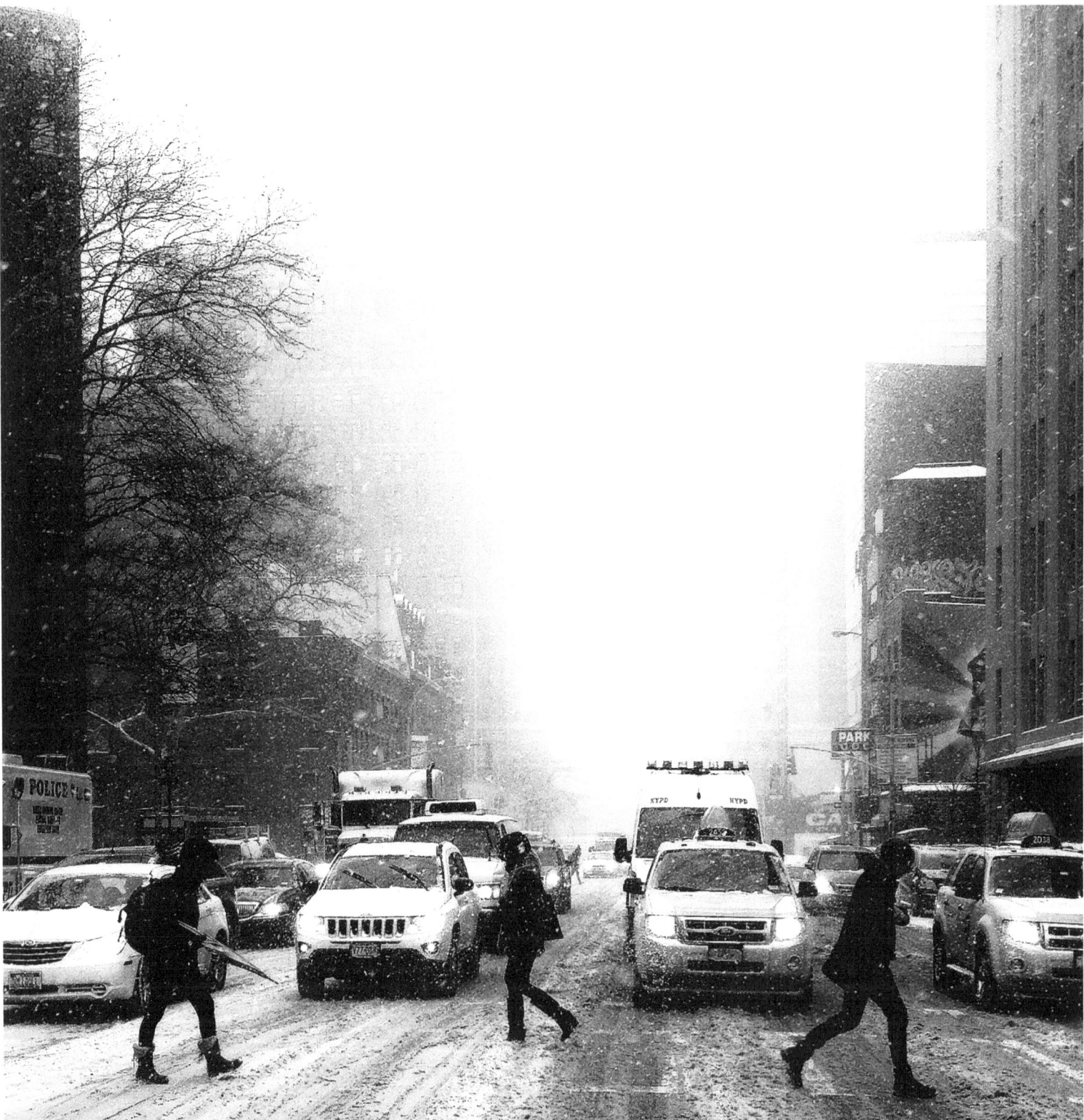

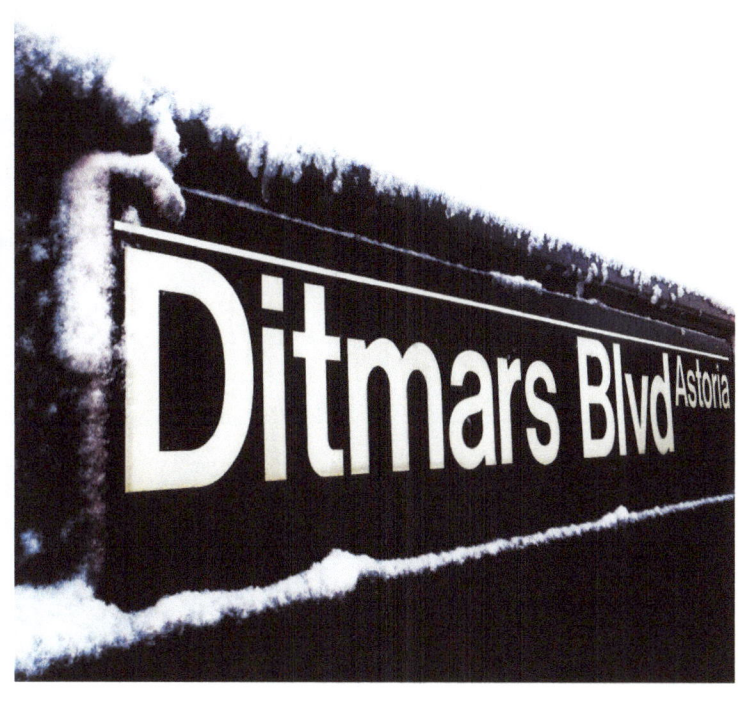

Winter can often be a struggle. Over our time in the concrete jungle we were pounded with not inches, but feet of snow.

In any other city in the world, snow is a manageable weather event. But when you have to walk to and from work, often times blocks on end, it quickly becomes one of the roughest parts of living in NYC.

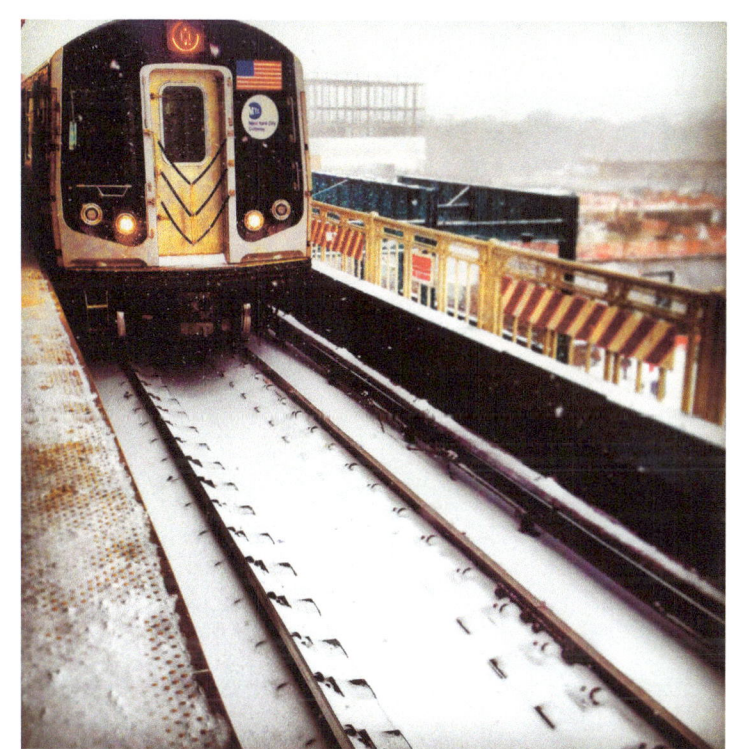

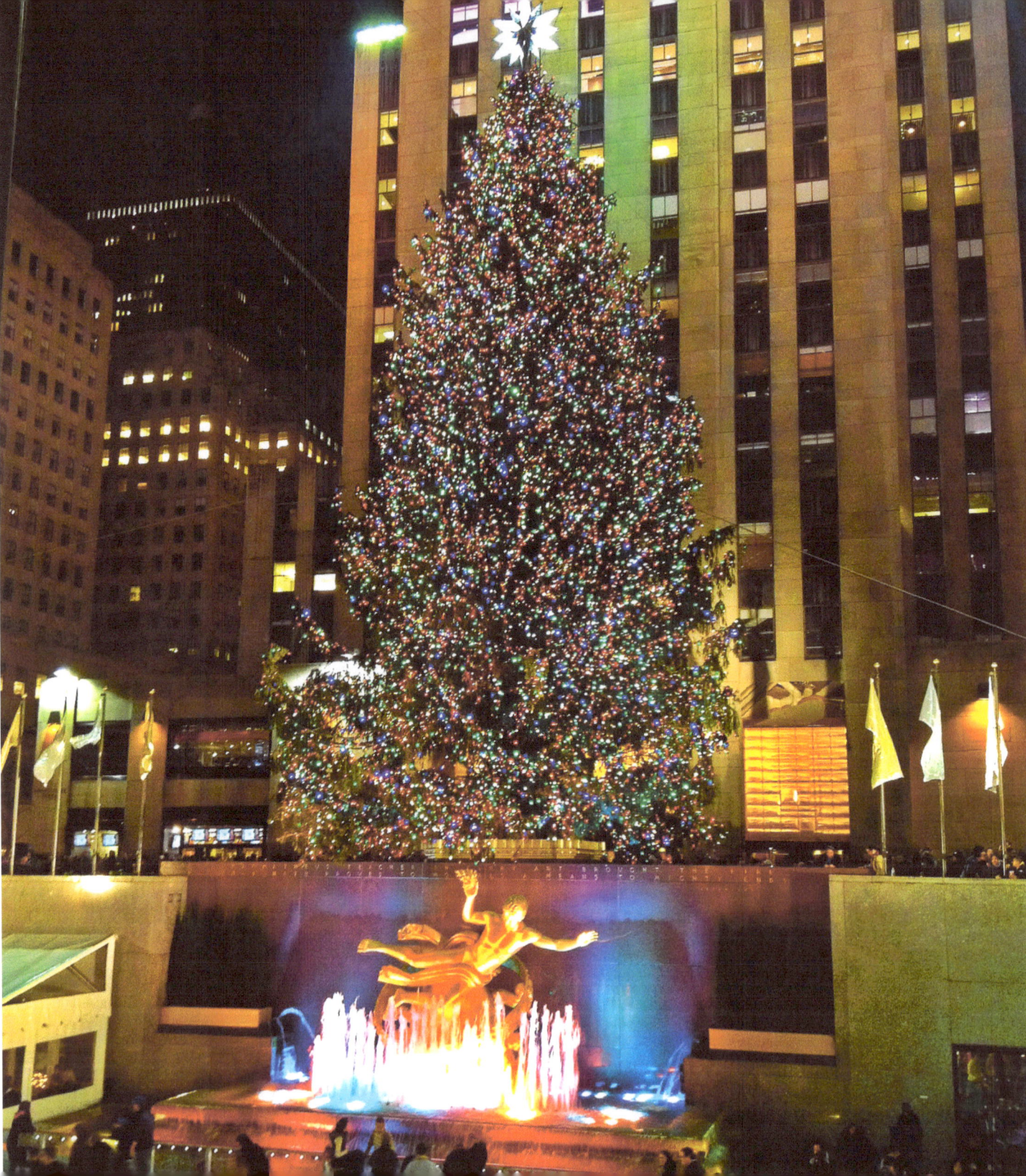

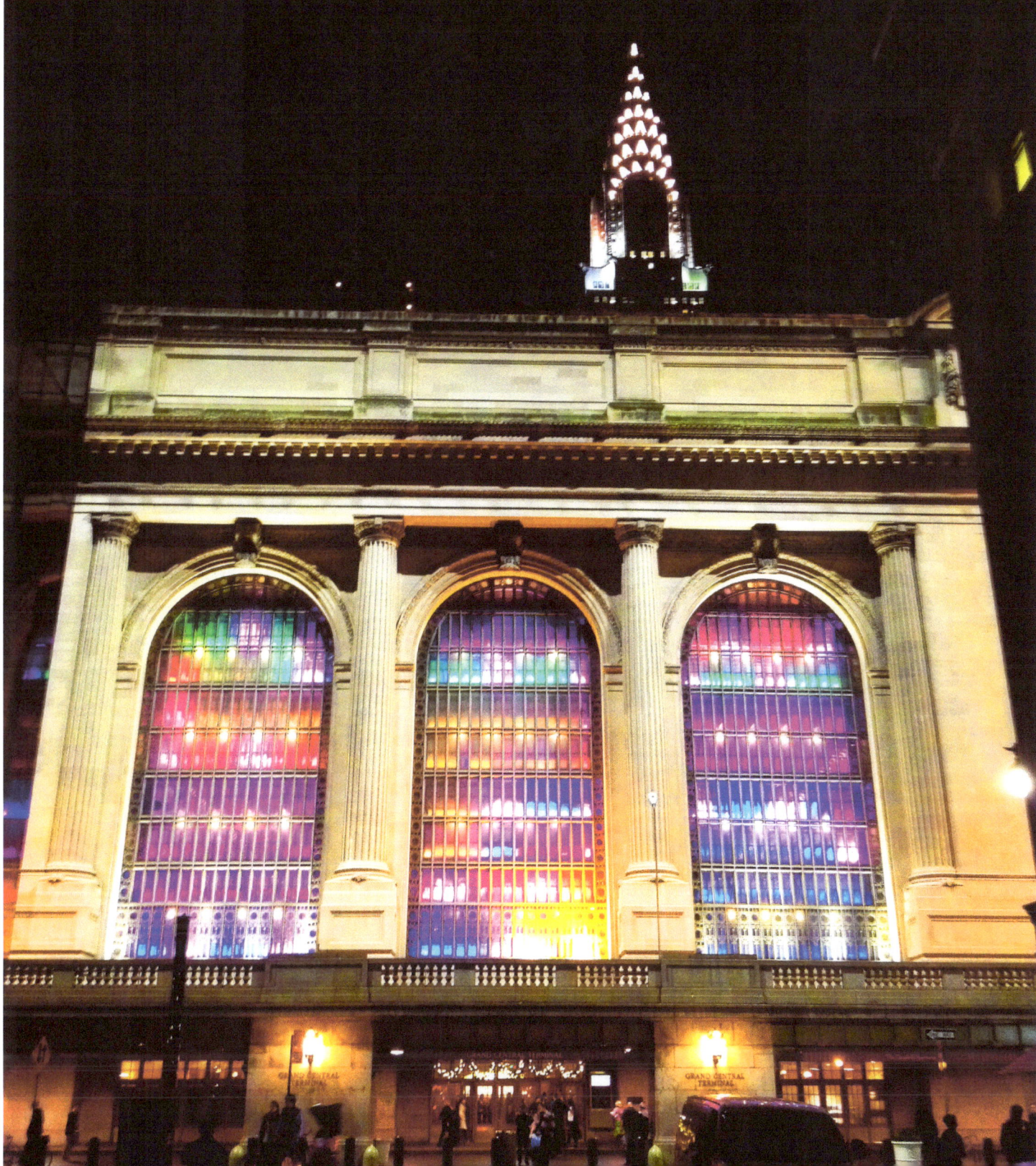

Spring

The beautiful spring came; and when Nature resumes her loveliness, the human soul is apt to revive also.

- Harriet Ann Jacobs

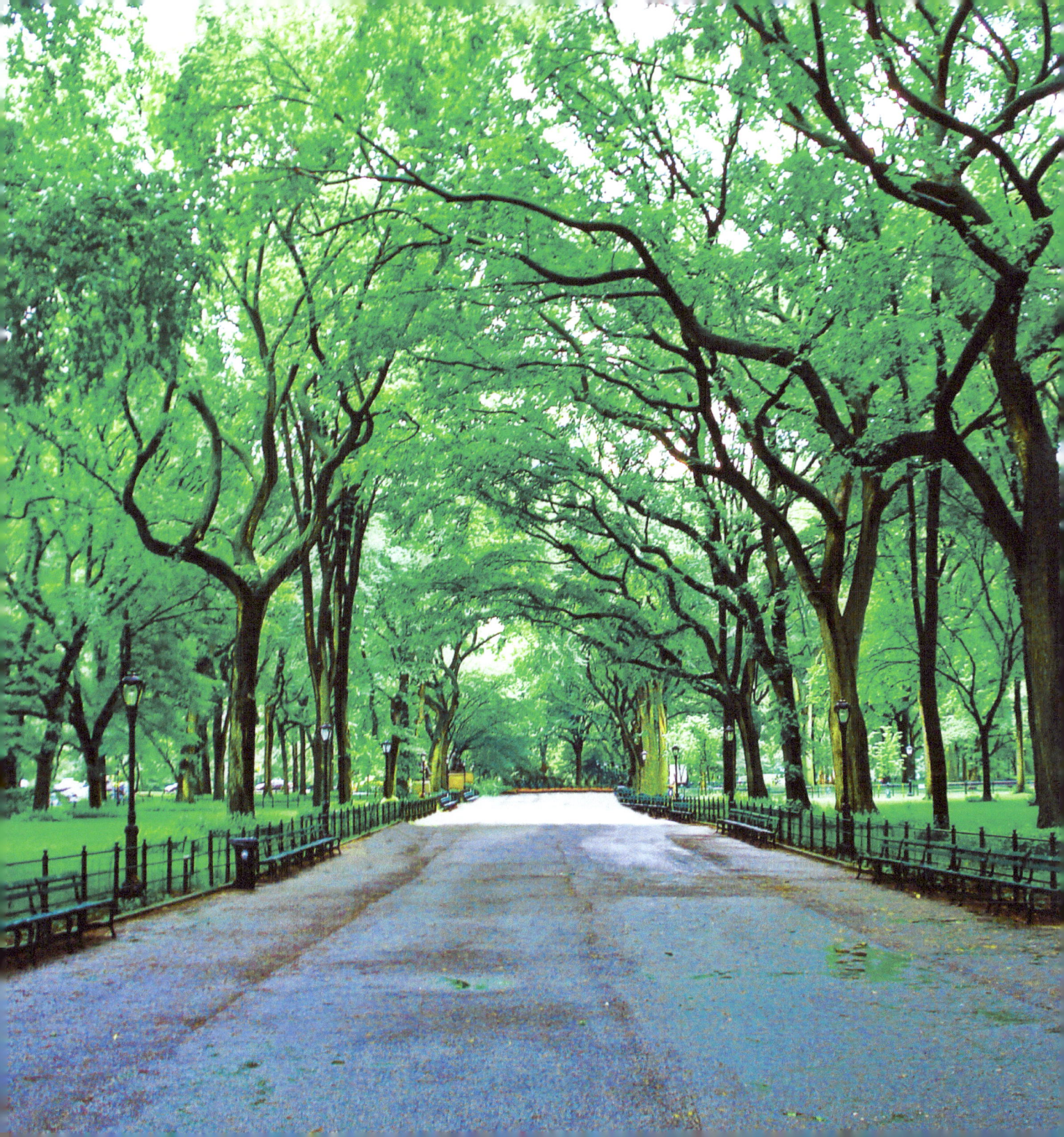

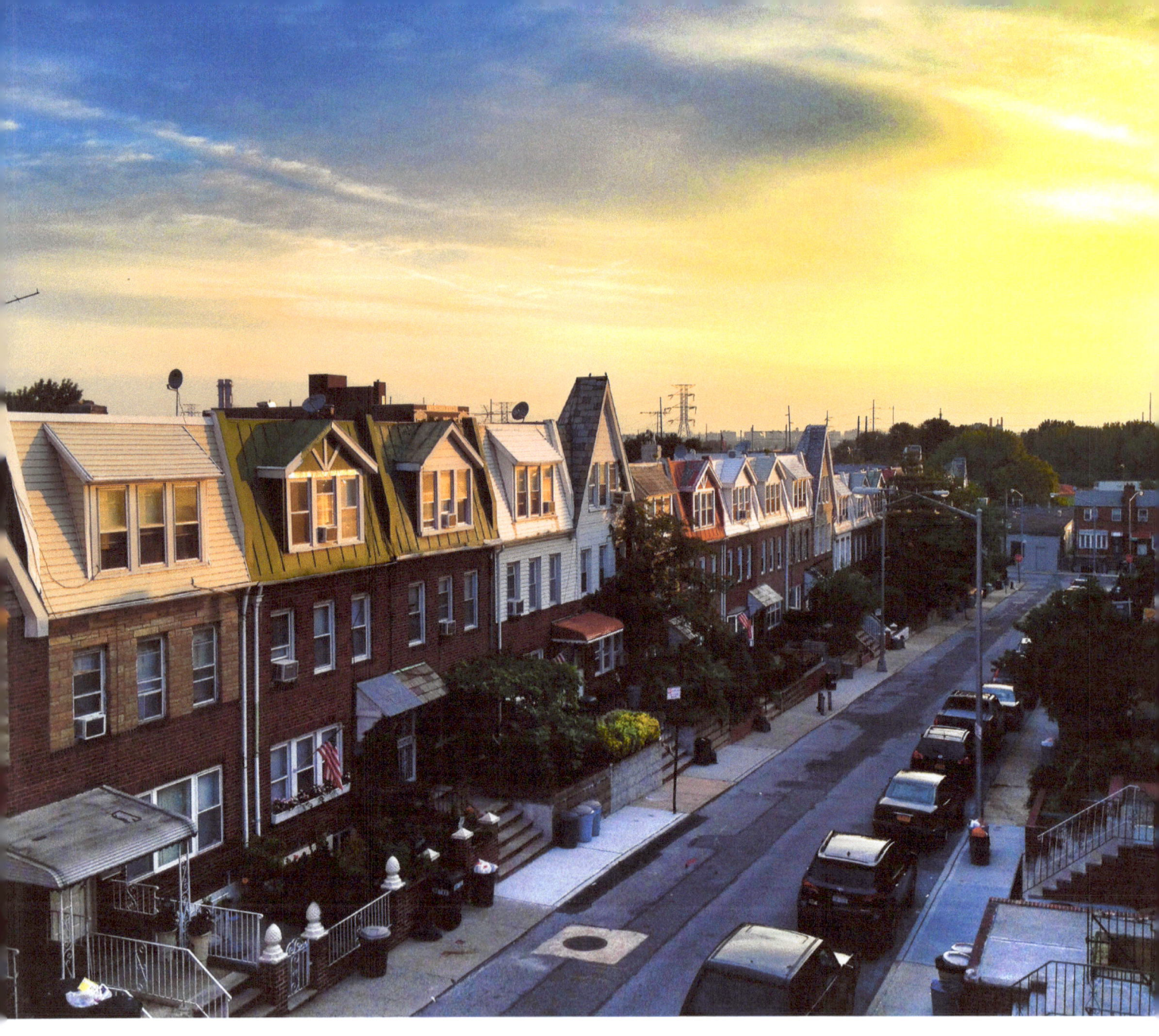

THE VIEW FROM OUR HOME
32nd STREET, ASTORIA

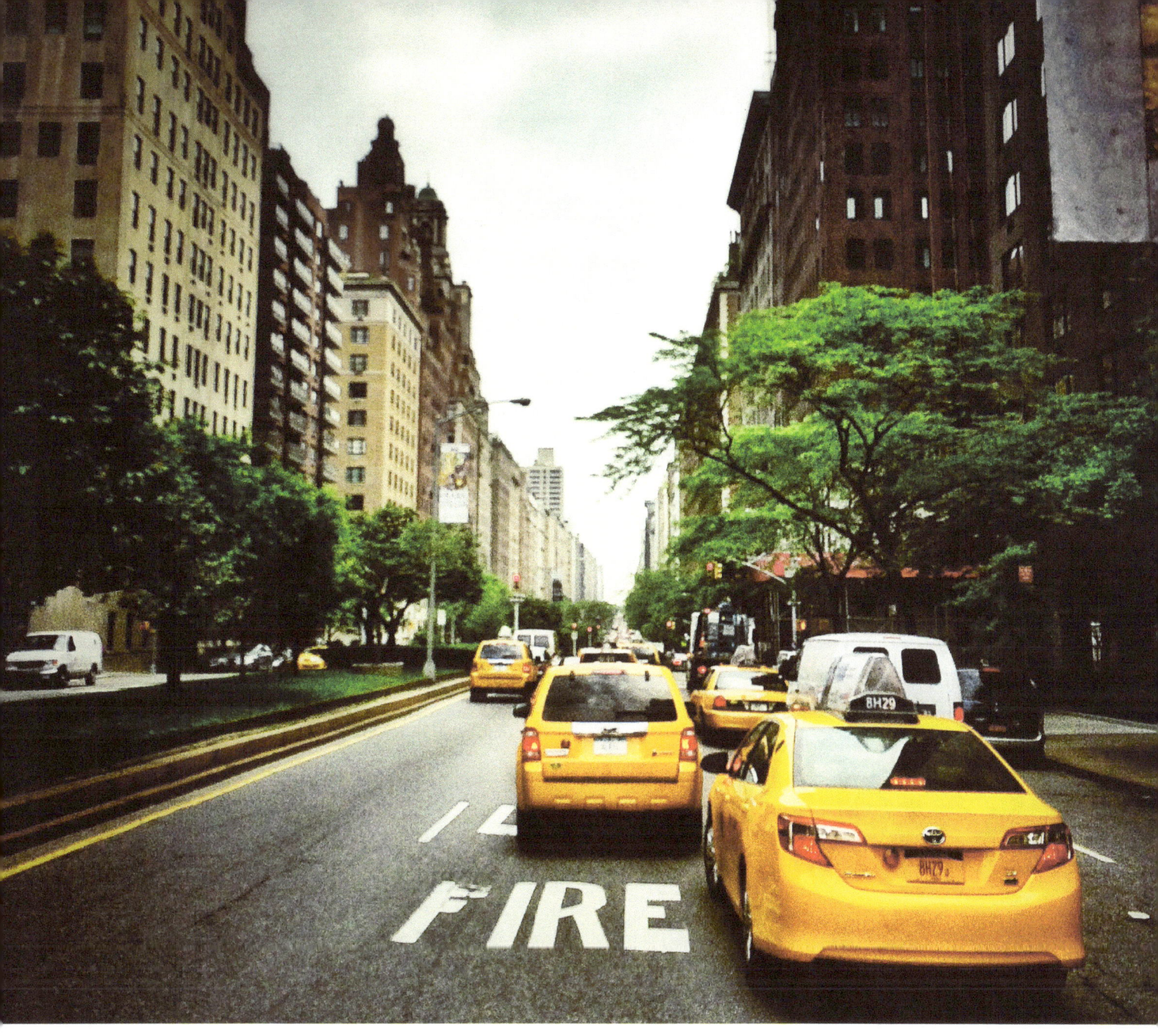

PARK AVENUE
UPPER EAST SIDE

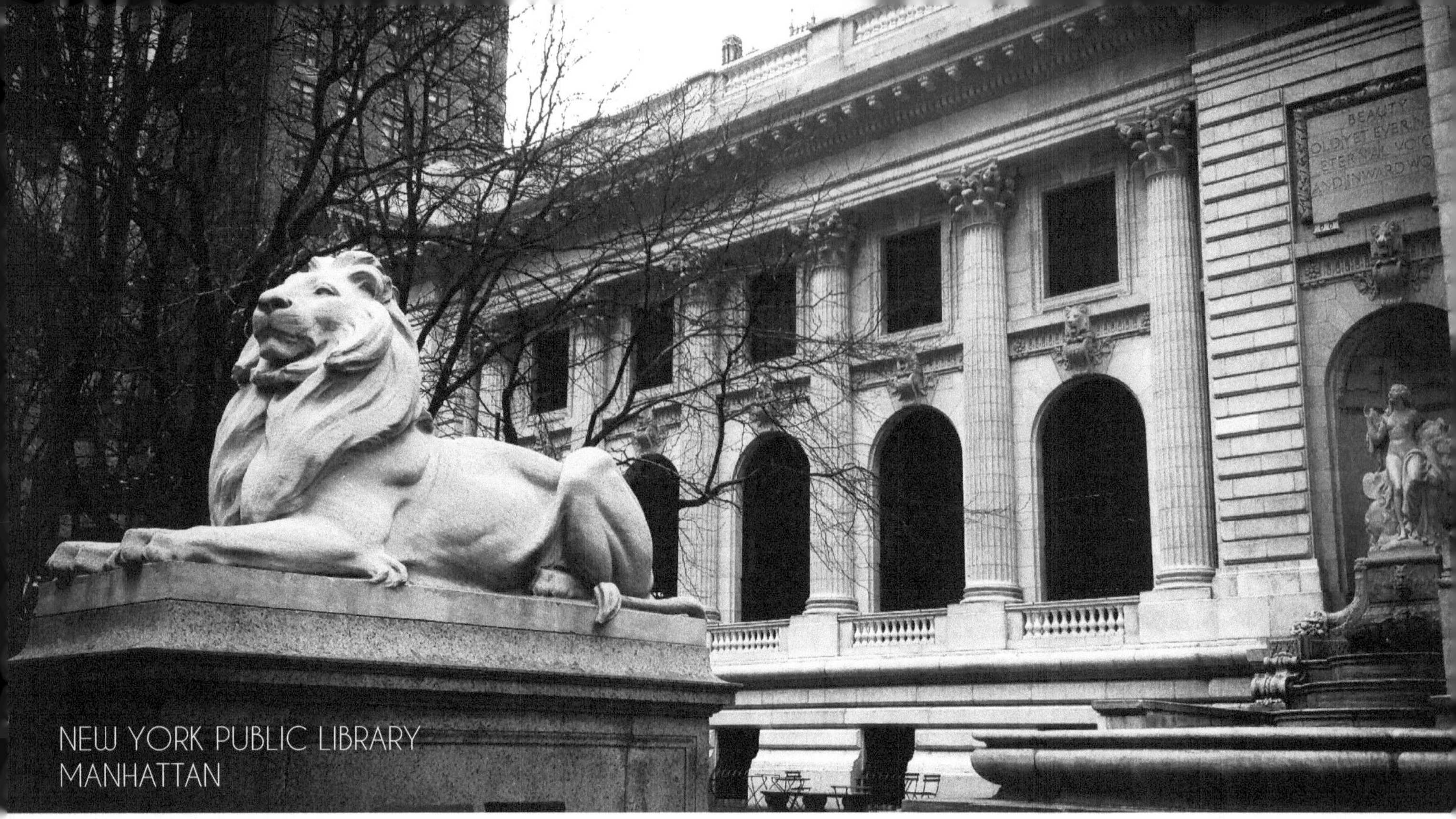

NEW YORK PUBLIC LIBRARY
MANHATTAN

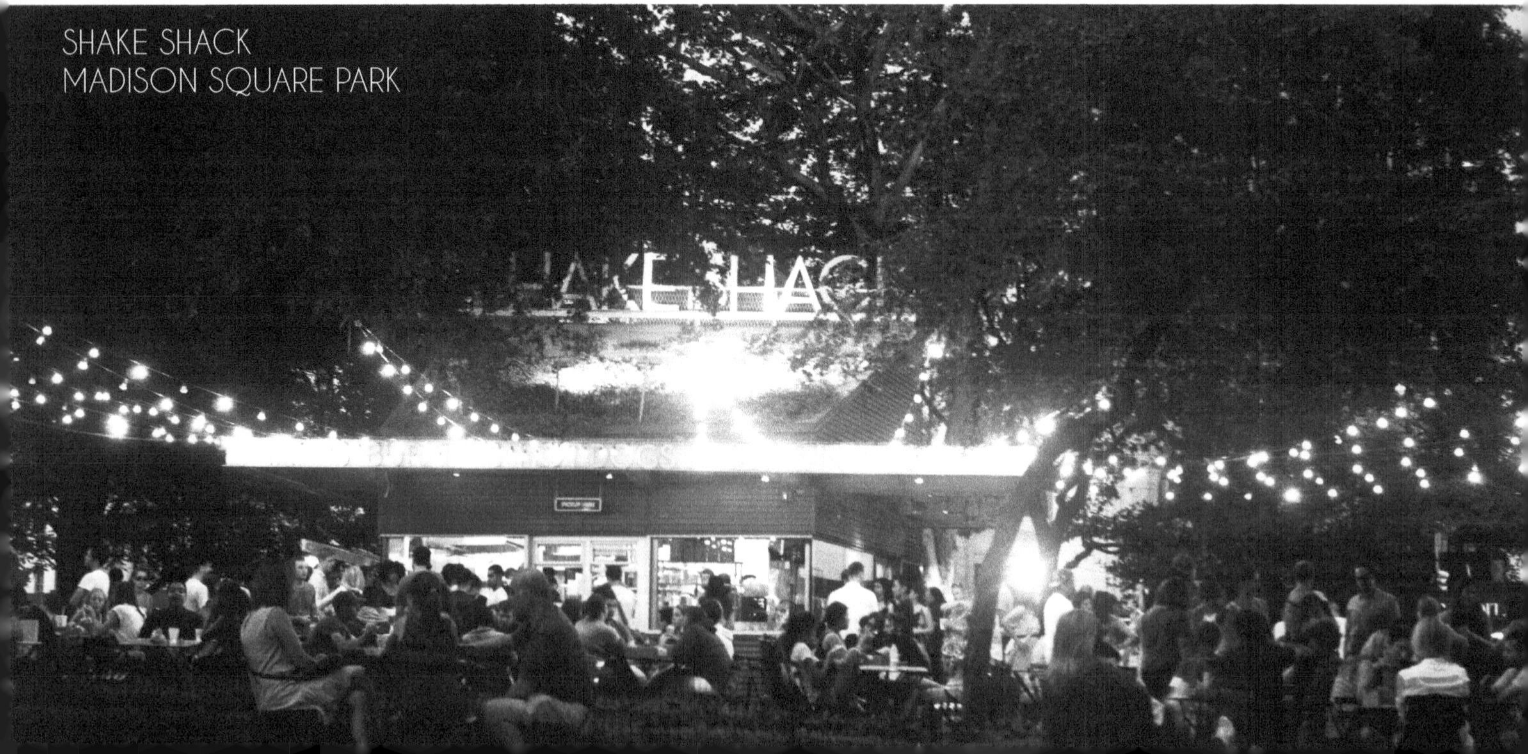

SHAKE SHACK
MADISON SQUARE PARK

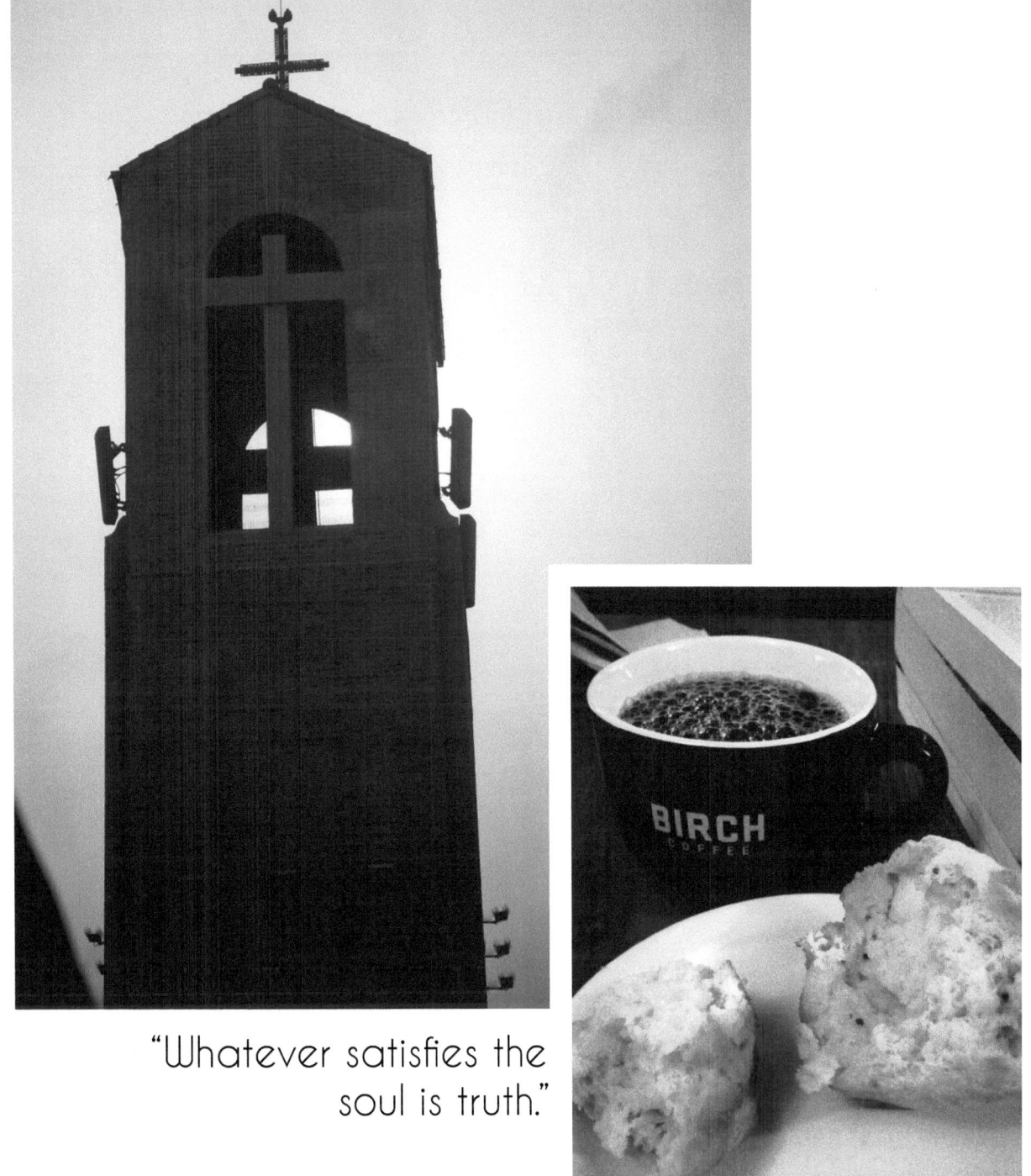

"Whatever satisfies the
soul is truth."

- Walt Whitman

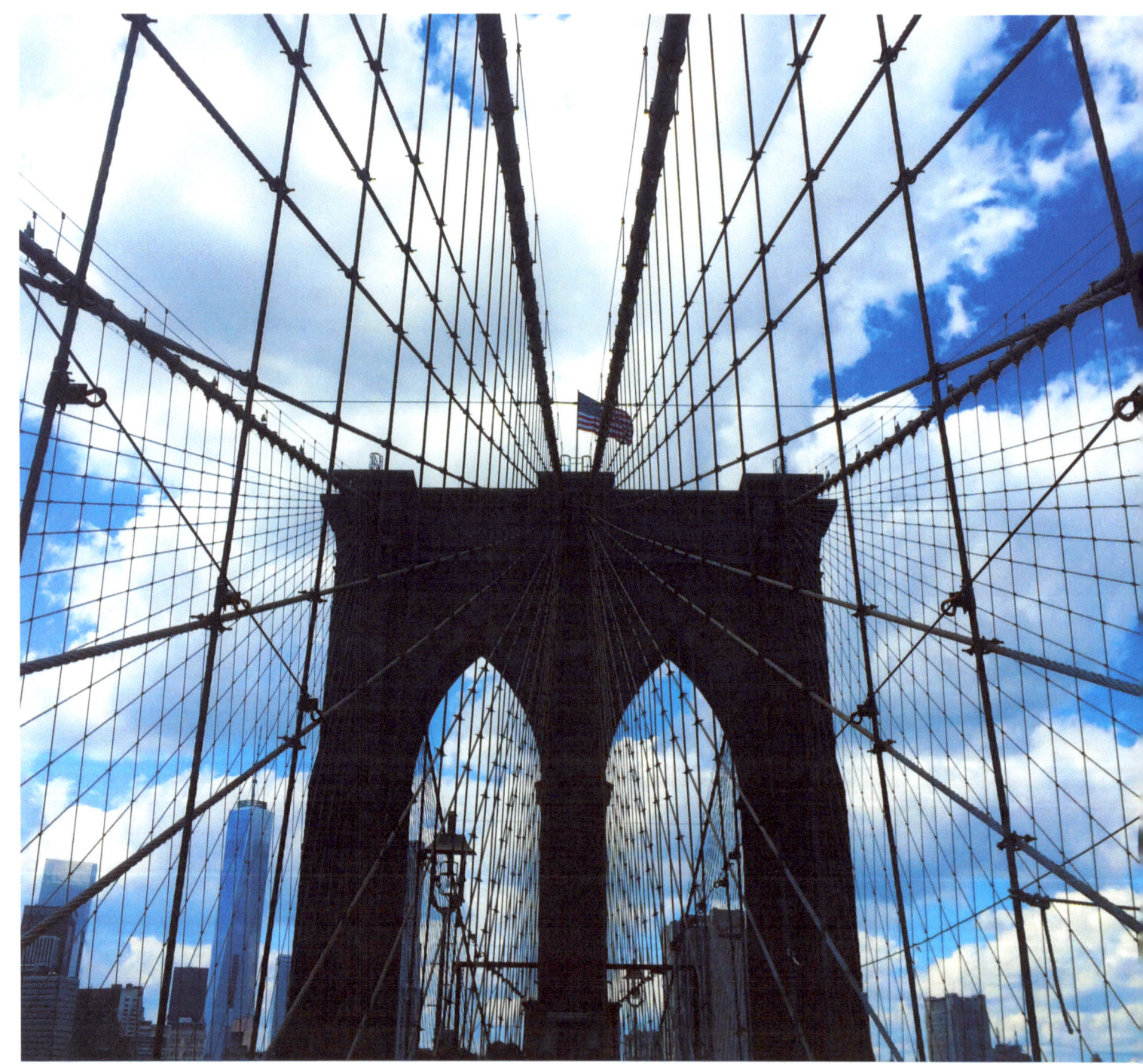

BROOKLYN BRIDGE

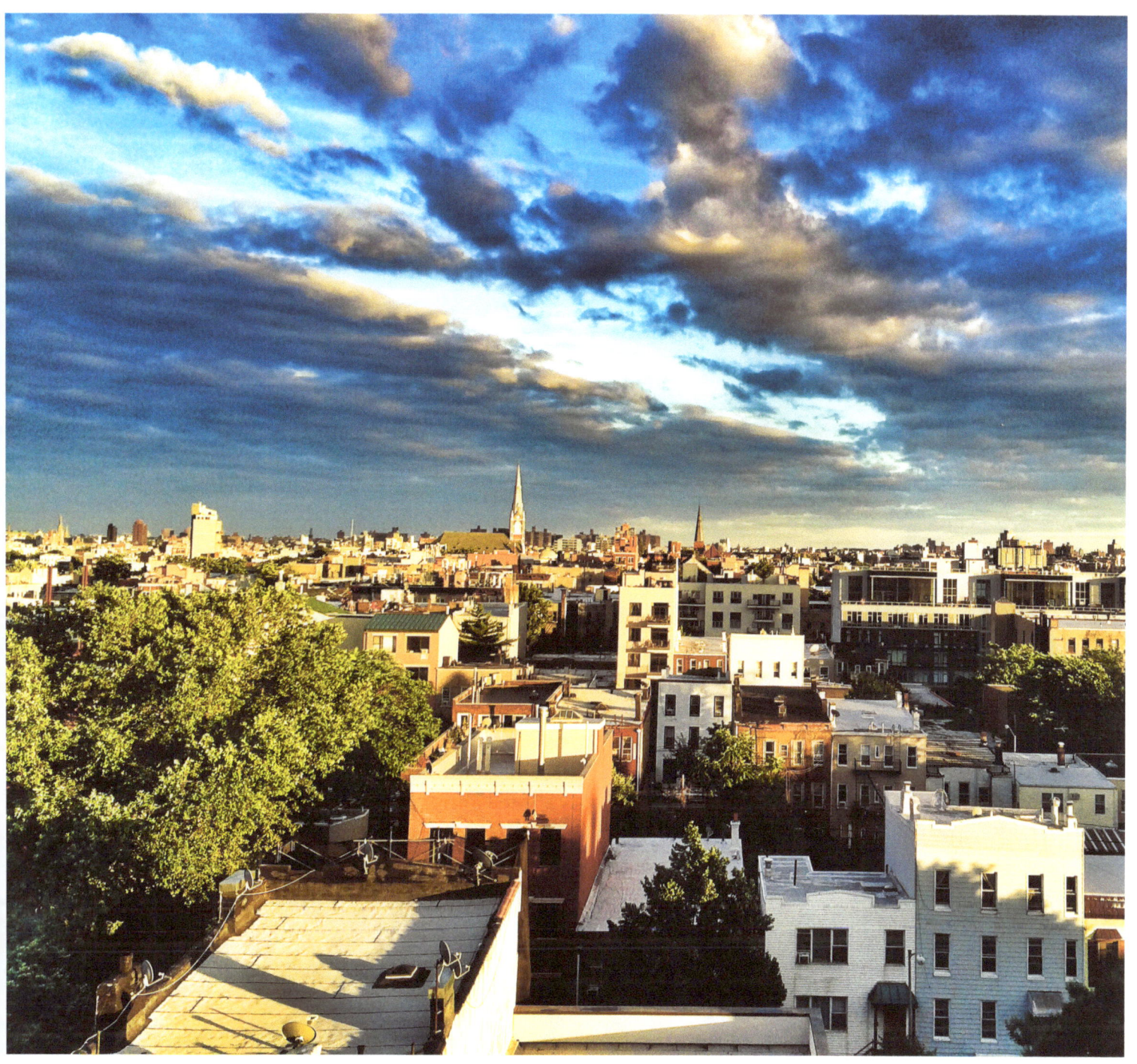

GREENPOINT, BROOKLYN

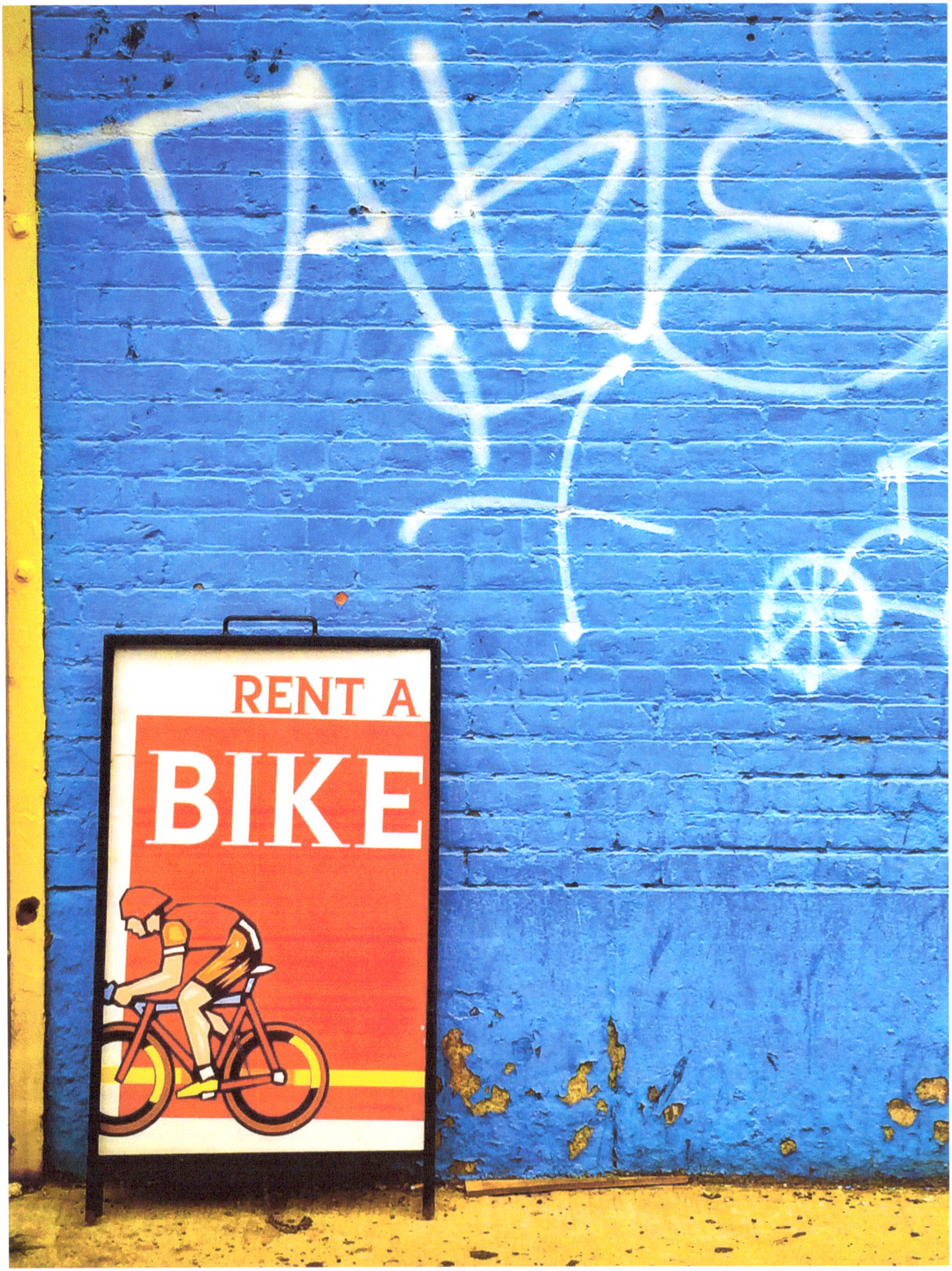

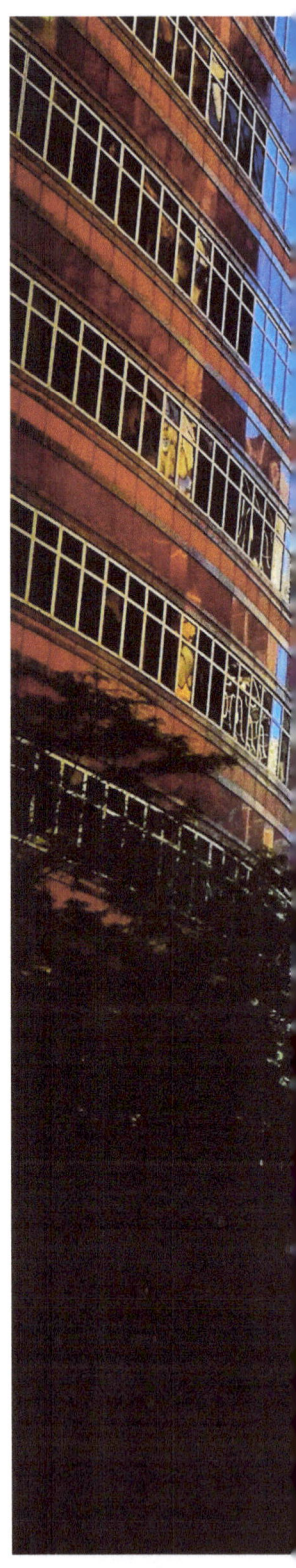

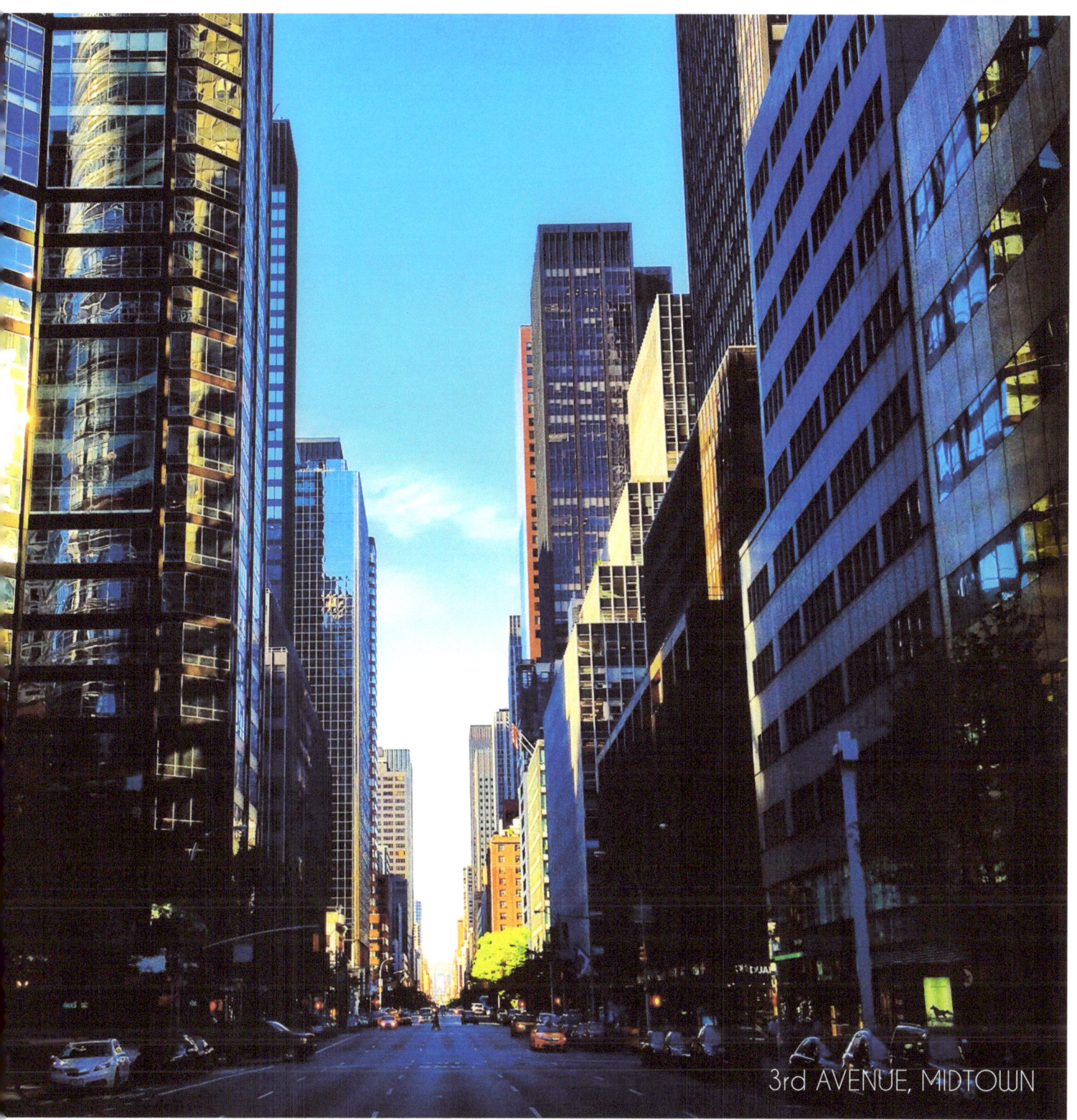

3rd AVENUE, MIDTOWN

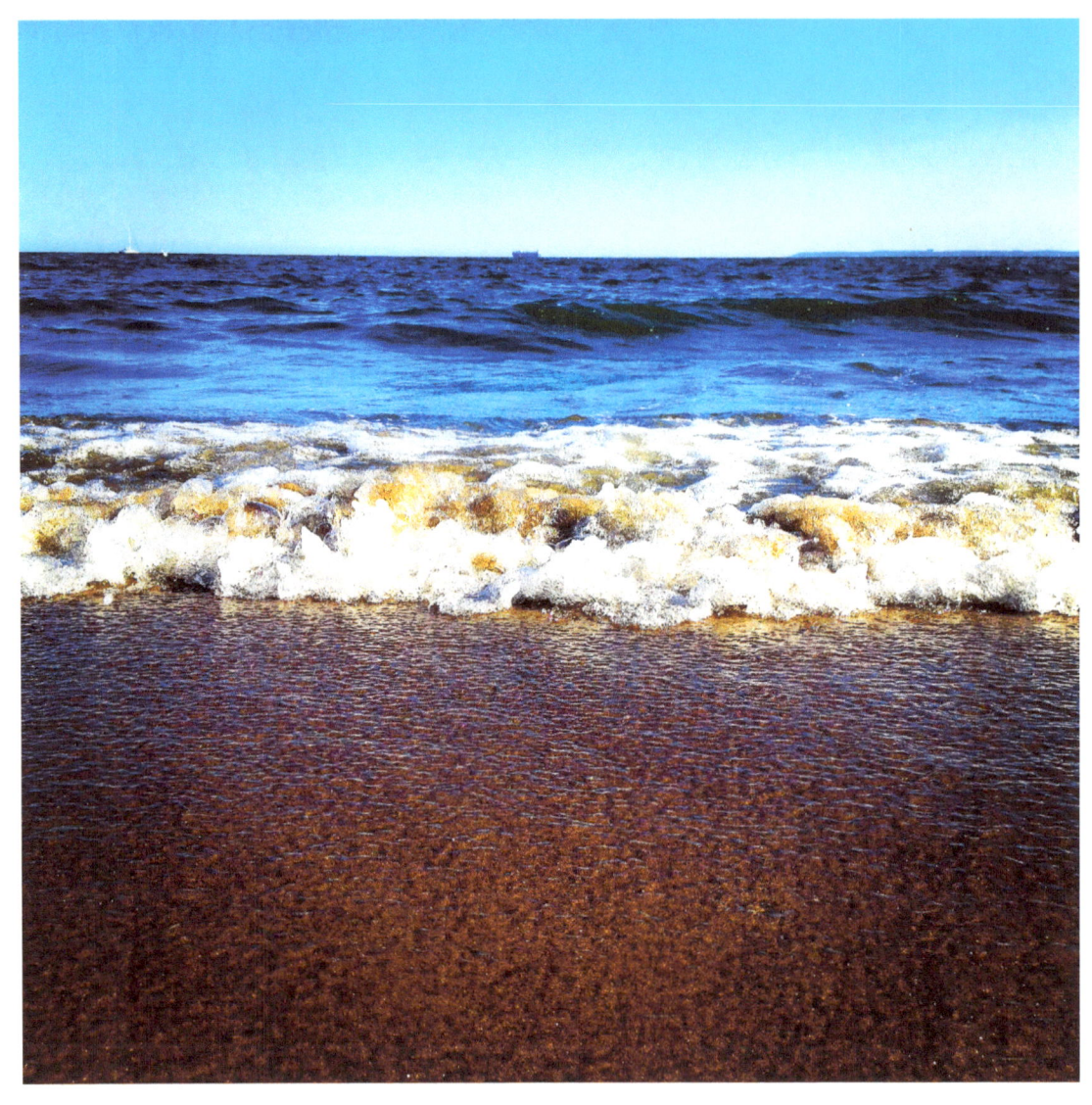

CONEY ISLAND BEACH

"At the end of the day, it isn't where I came from ...

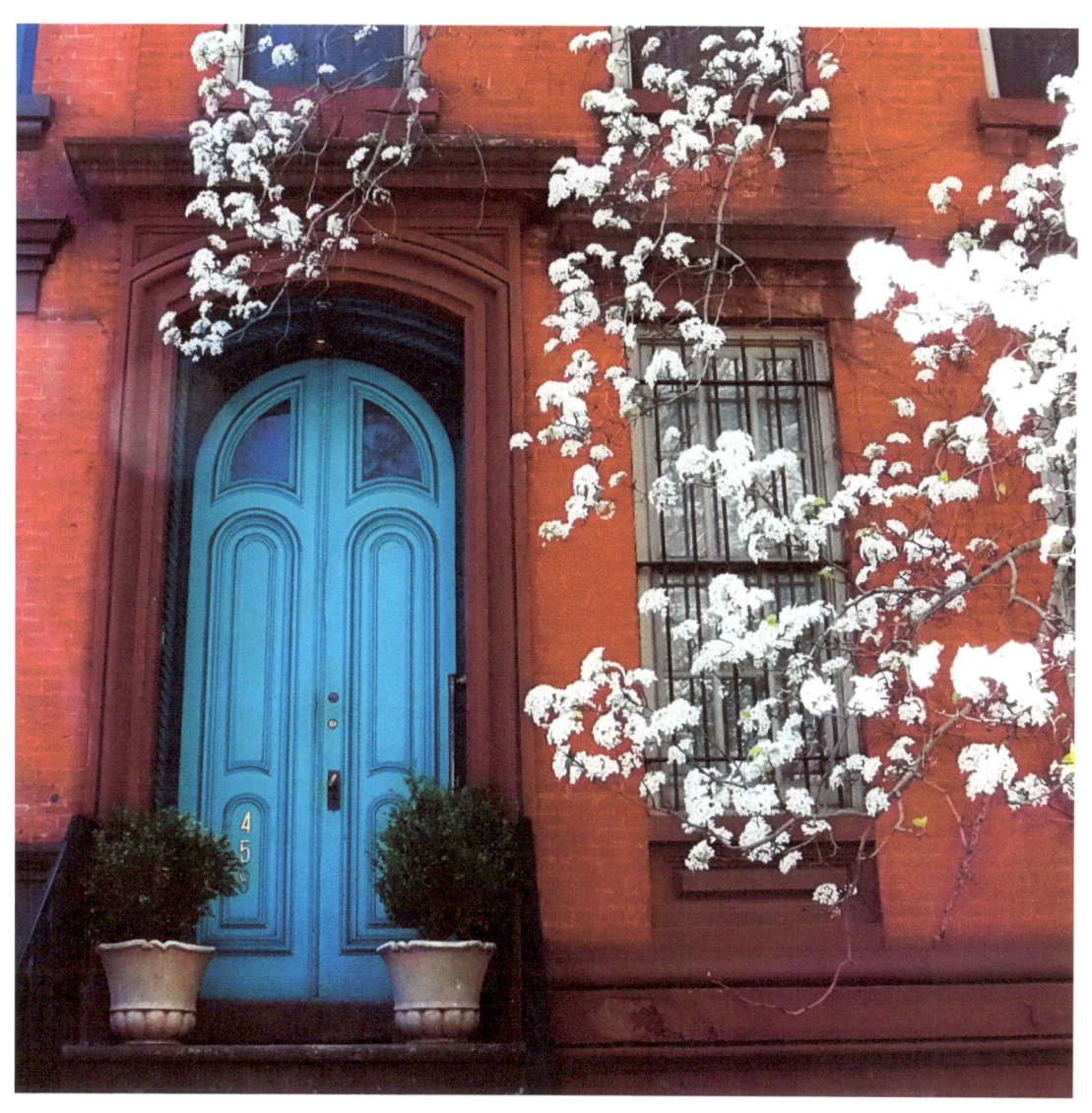

25th STREET, CHELSEA

... Maybe home is somewhere I'm going and never have been before."

- Warsan Shire

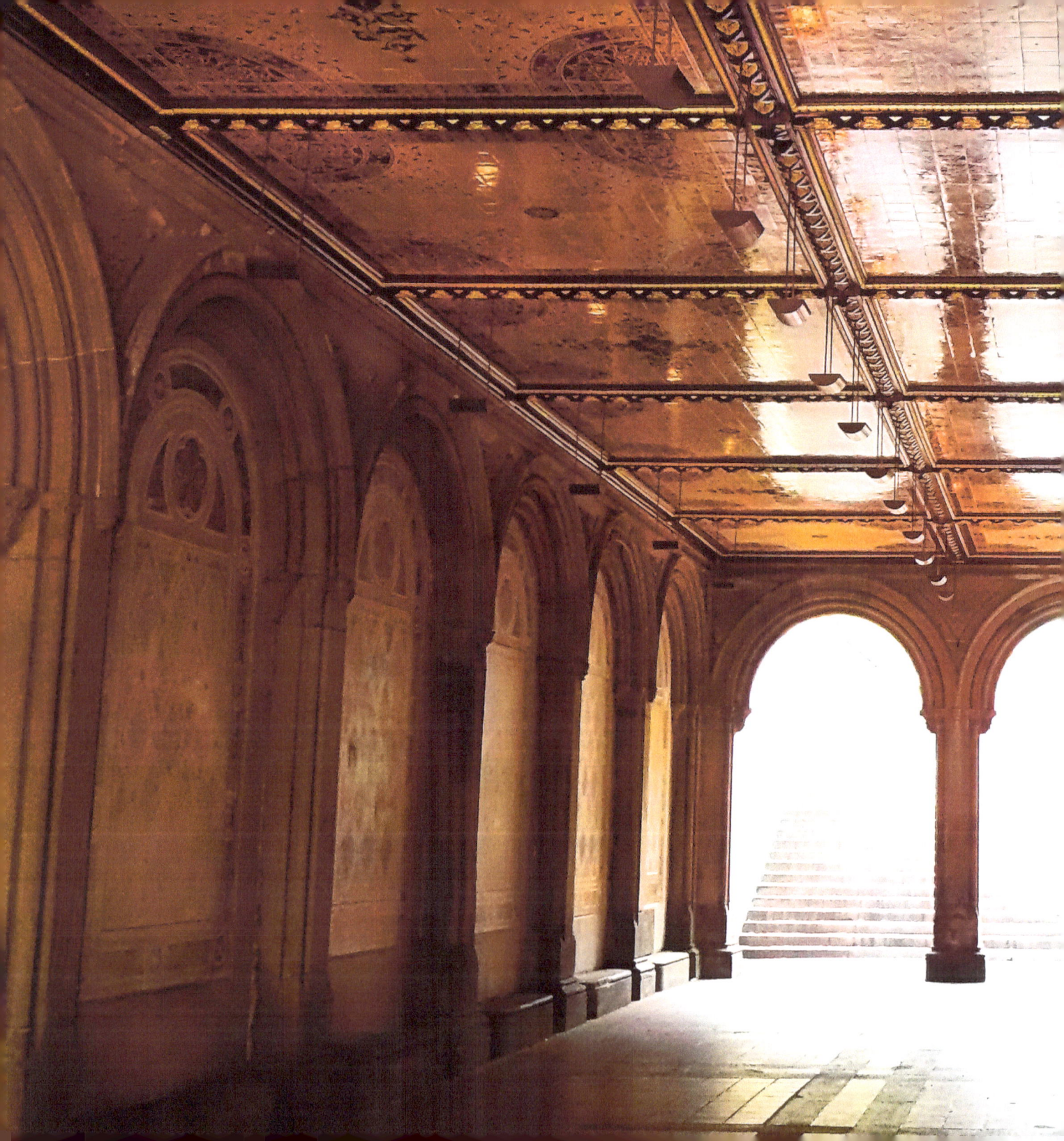

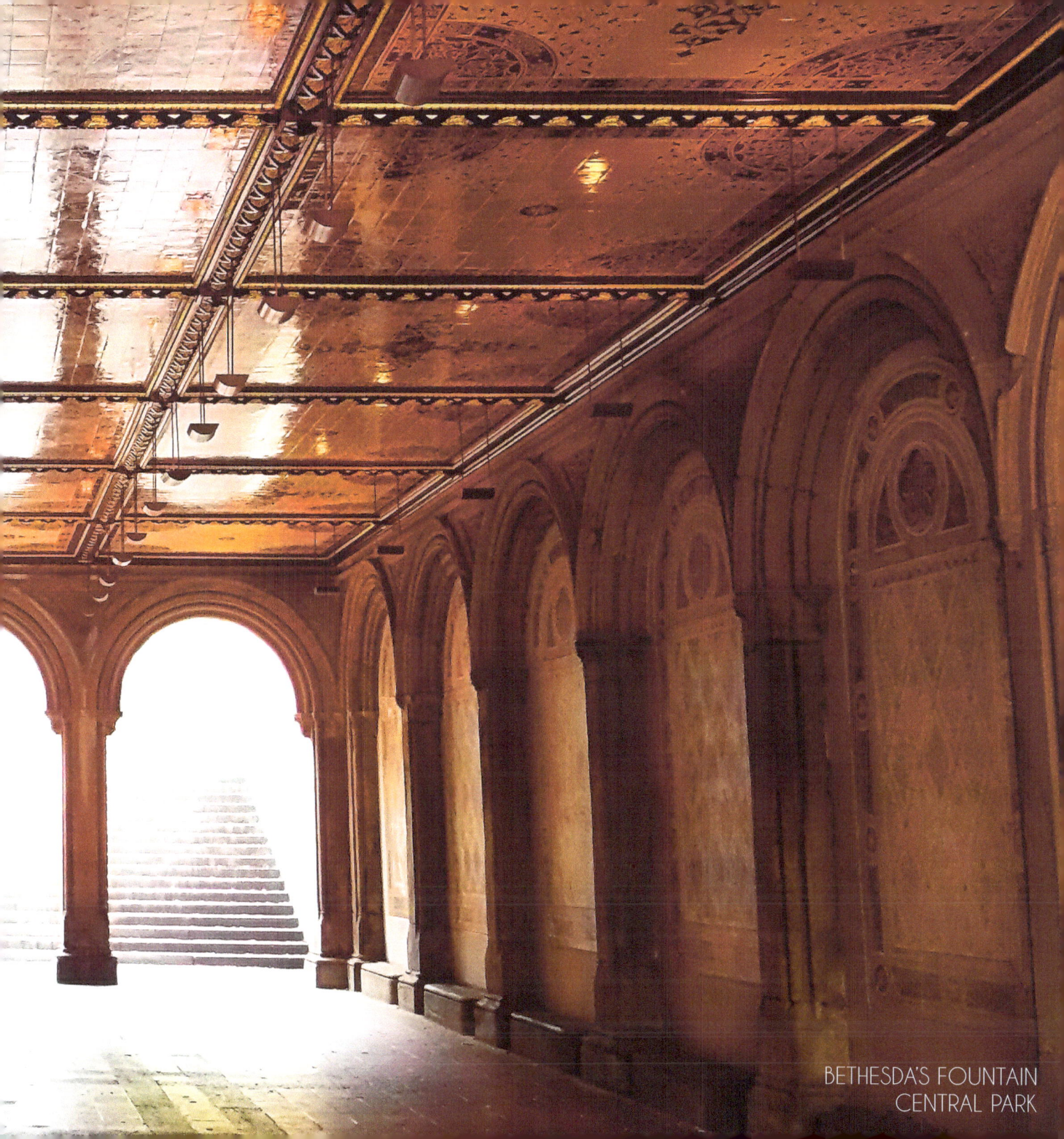

BETHESDA'S FOUNTAIN
CENTRAL PARK

Summer

"I love New York on summer afternoons when every one's away. There's something very sensuous about it - overripe, as if all sorts of funny fruits were going to fall into your hands."

— F. Scott Fitzgerald

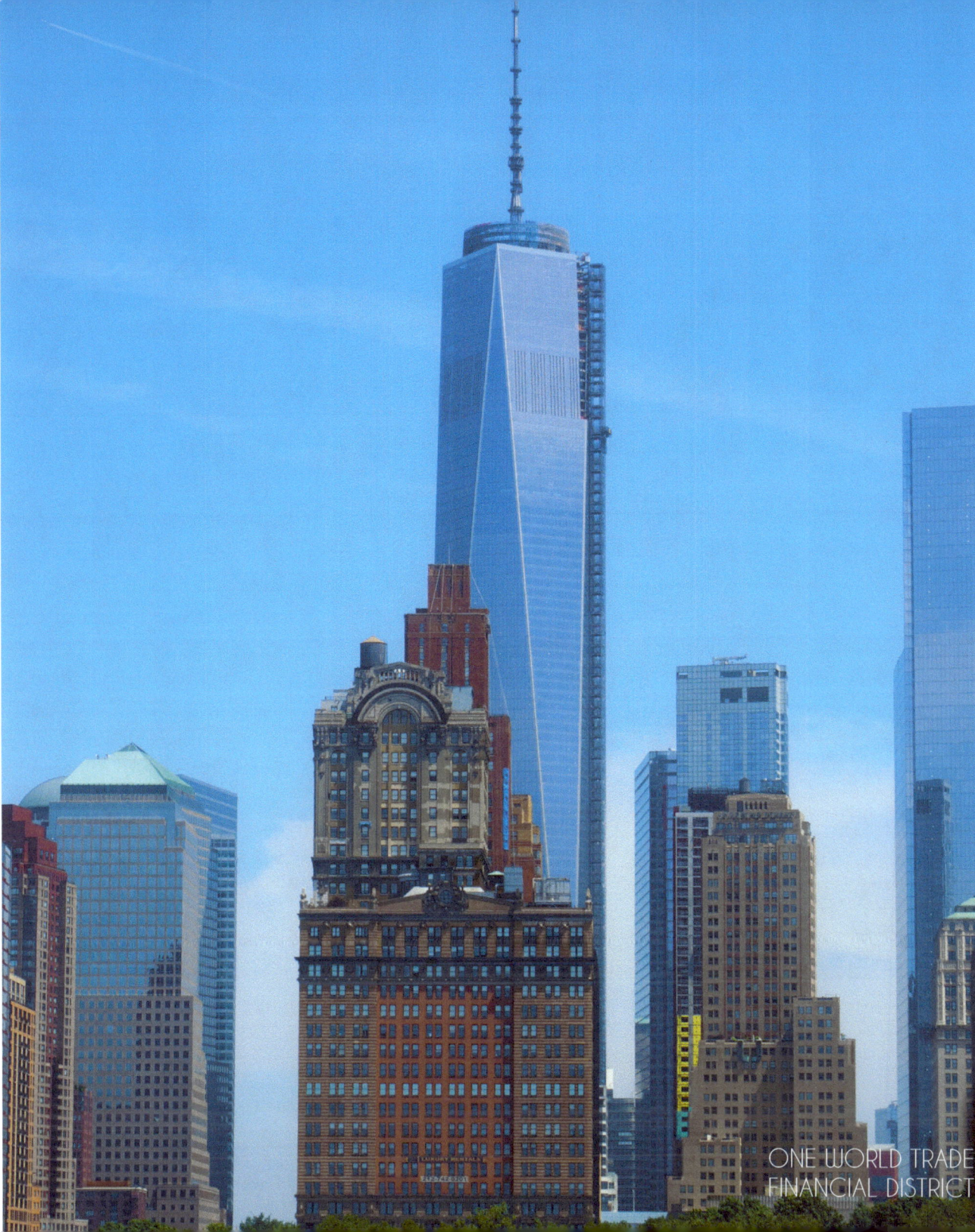

ONE WORLD TRADE
FINANCIAL DISTRICT

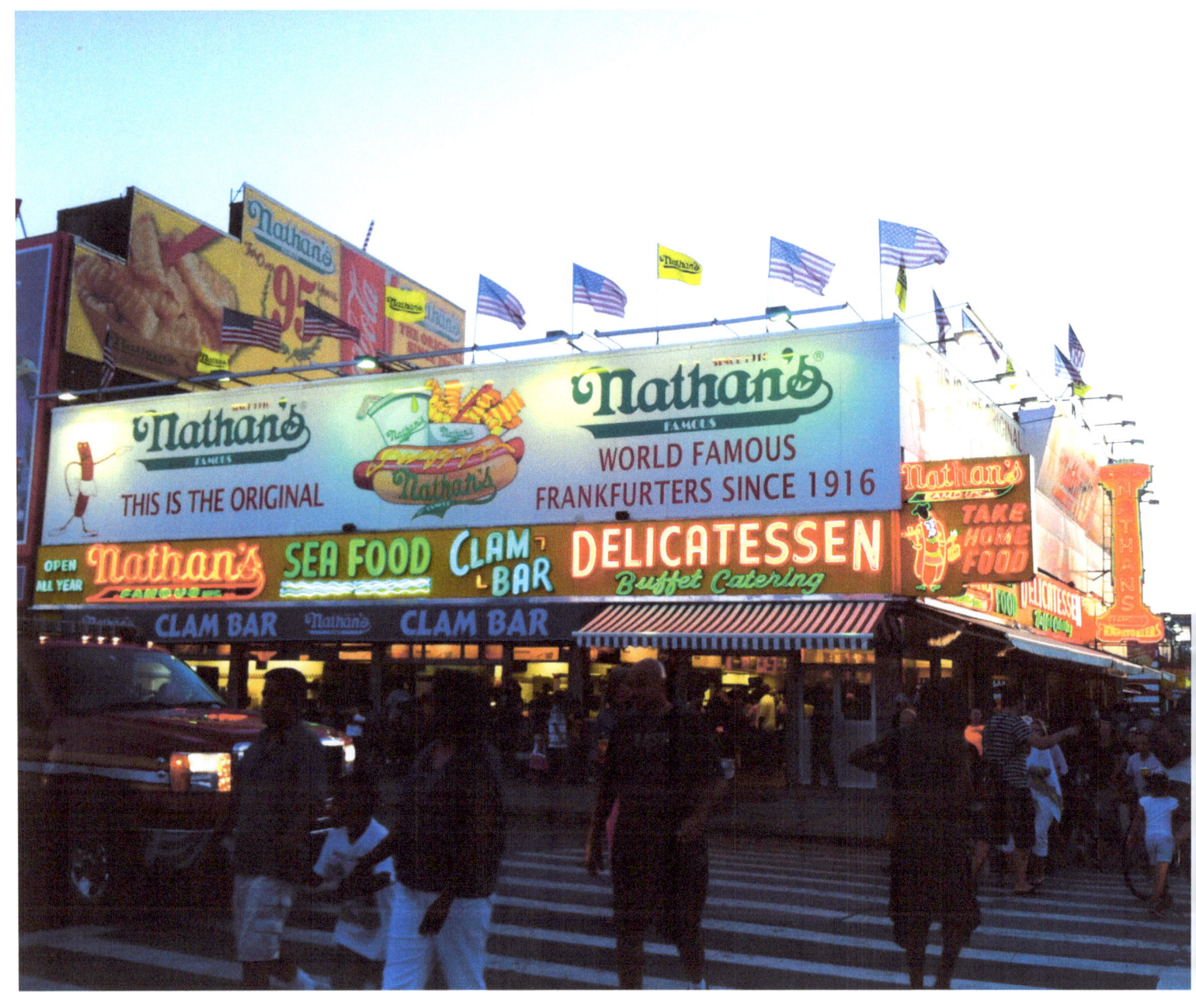

NATHAN'S FAMOUS
CONEY ISLAND, BROOKLYN

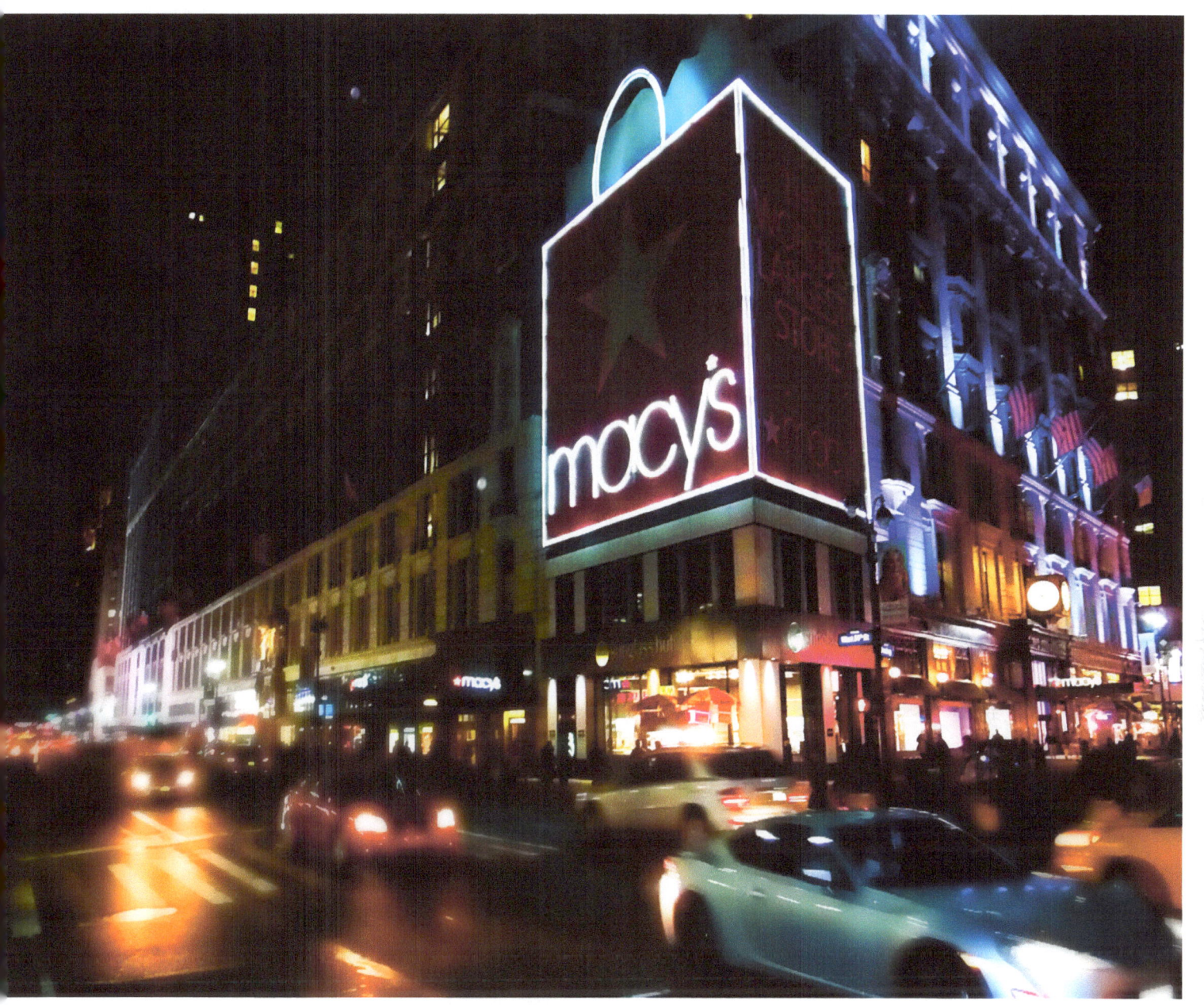

34th STREET MACY'S
MIDTOWN

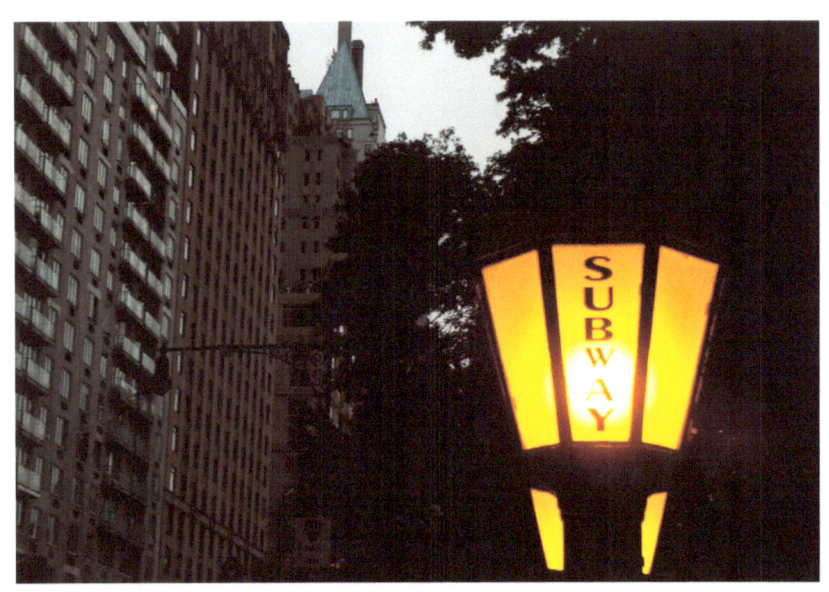

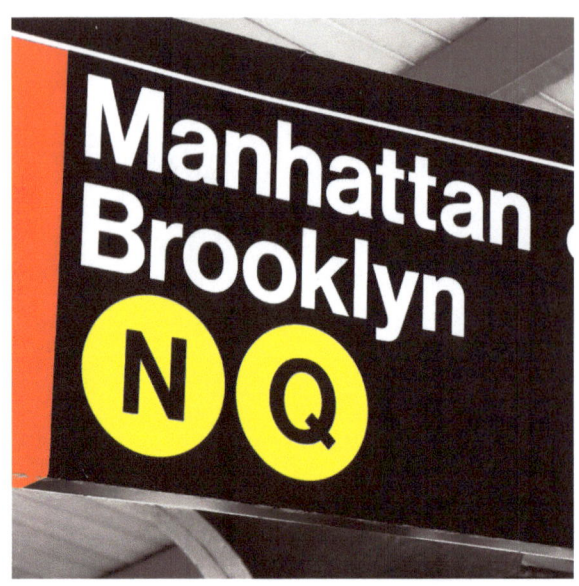

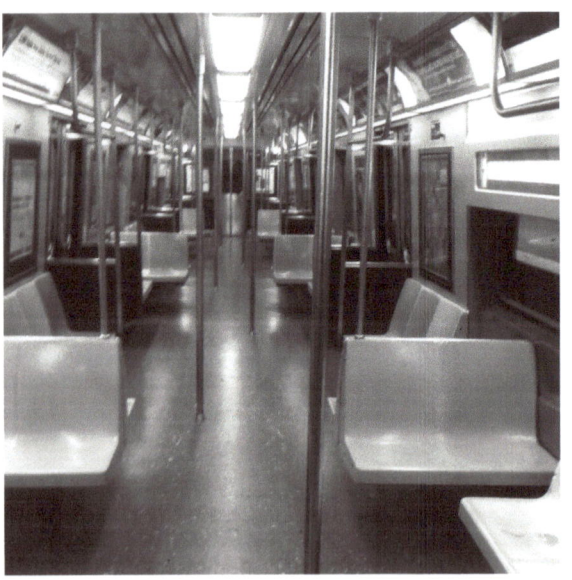

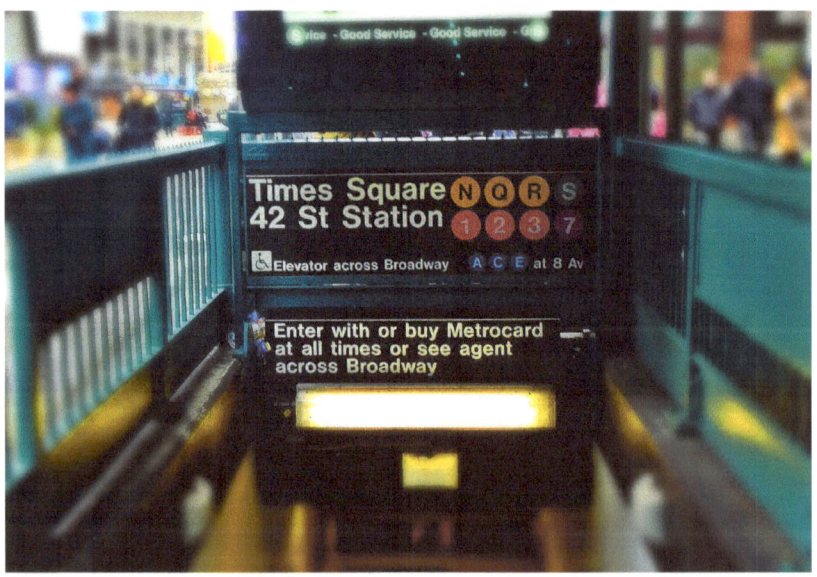

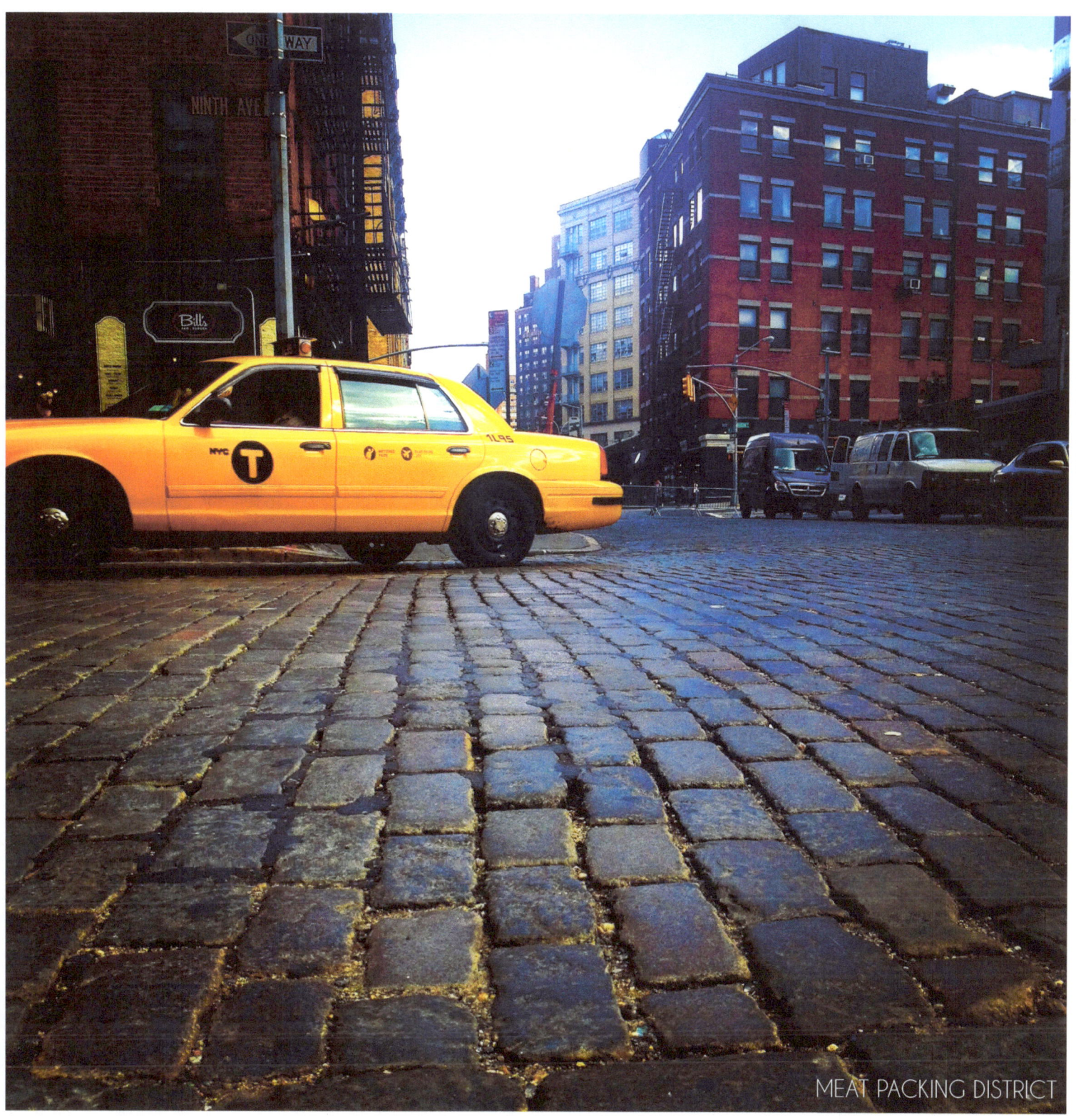

MEAT PACKING DISTRICT

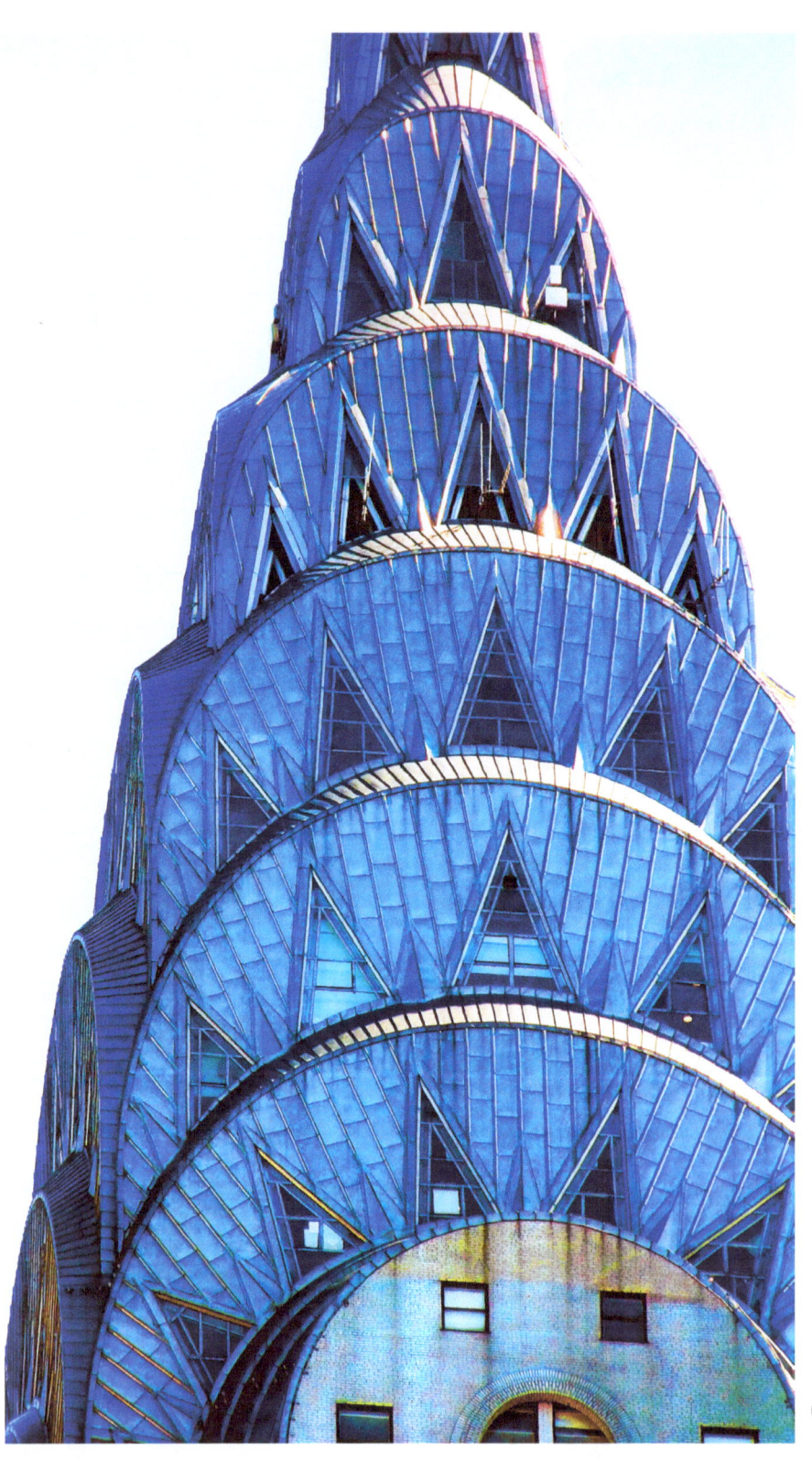

New York City is full of iconic buildings and landmarks. Without even knowing it, these famous façades become your daily view, your source of inspiration, and even your beacon, leading you home after a long day of chasing the dream.

CHRYSLER BUILDING

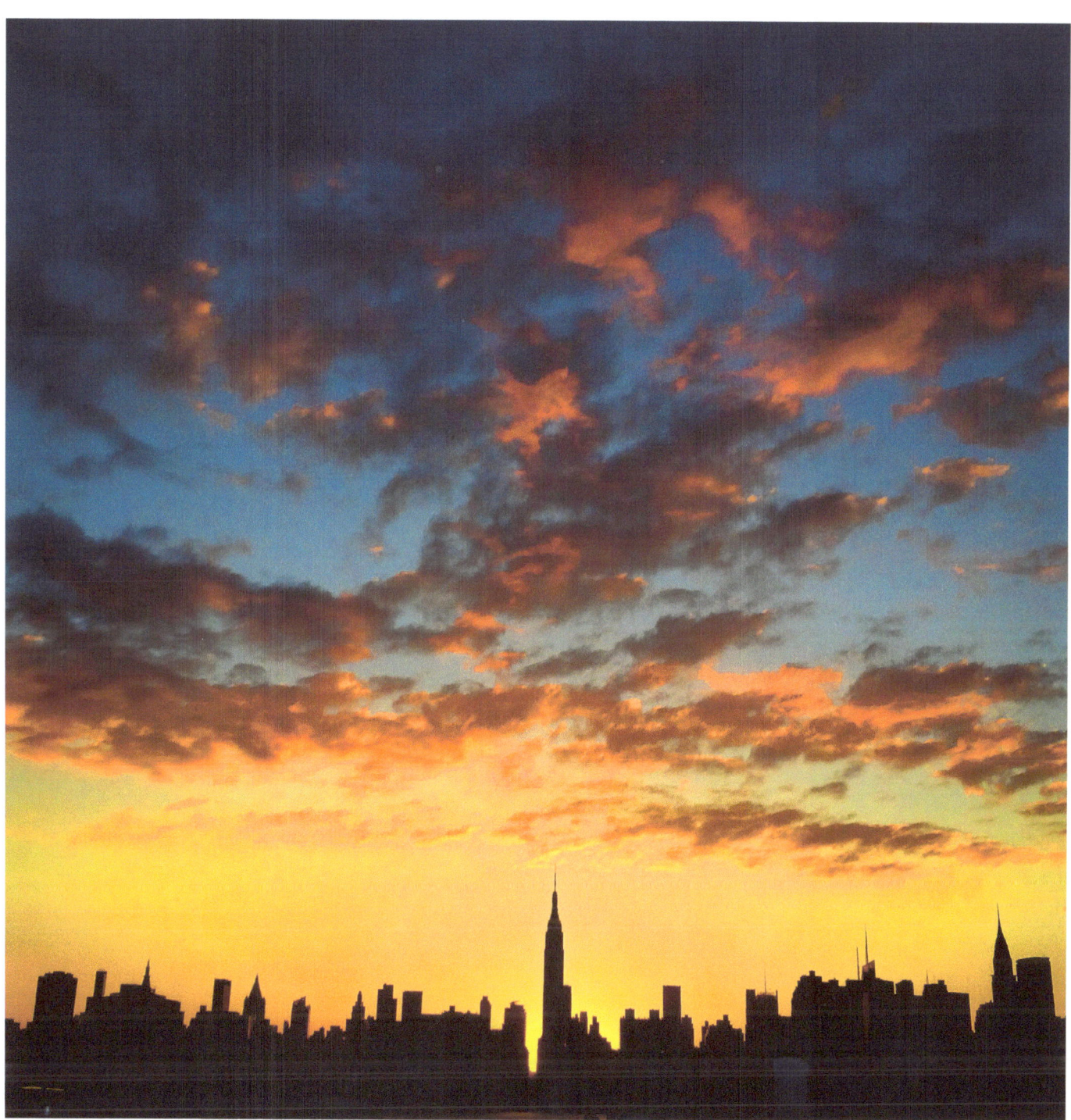

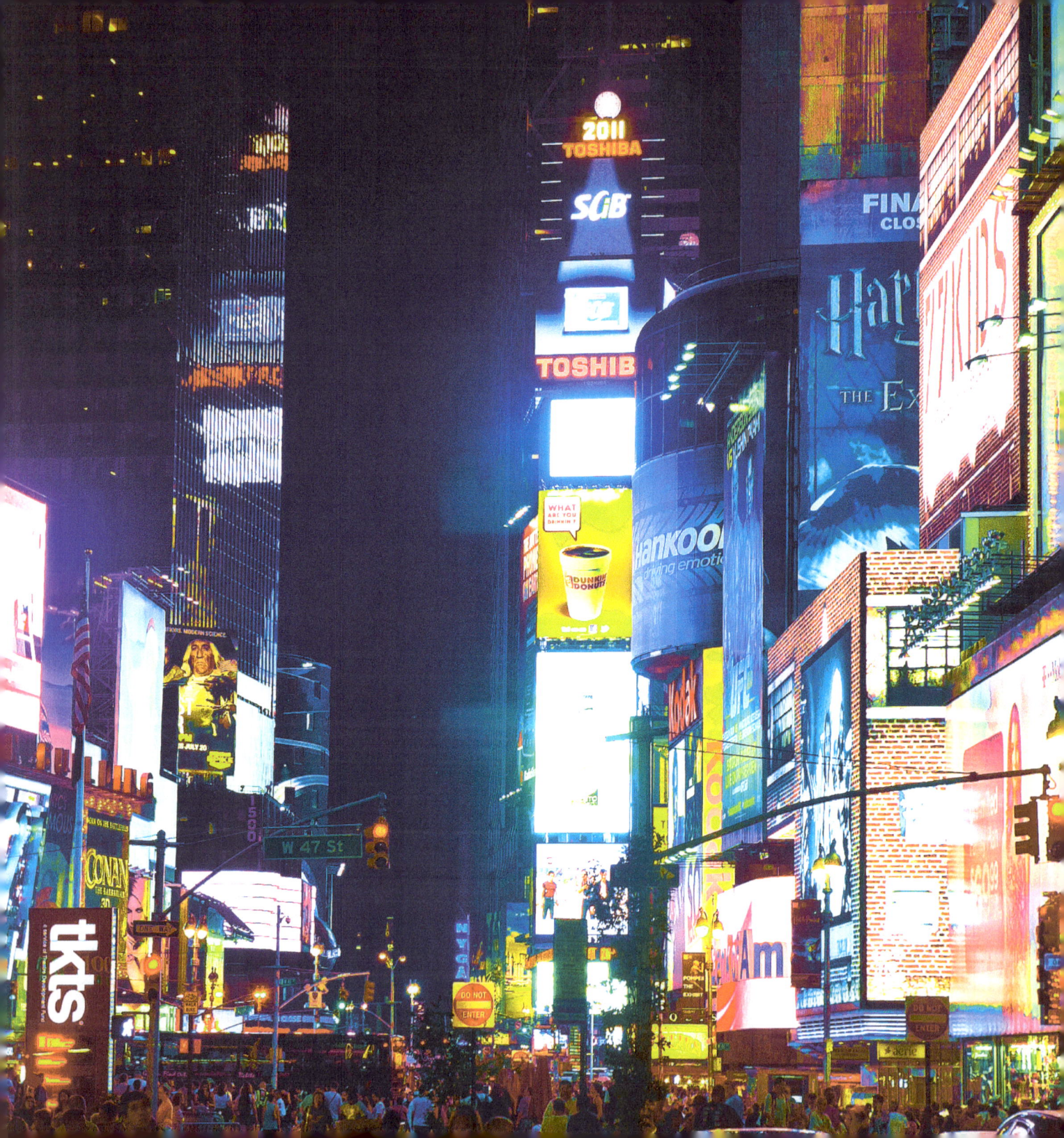

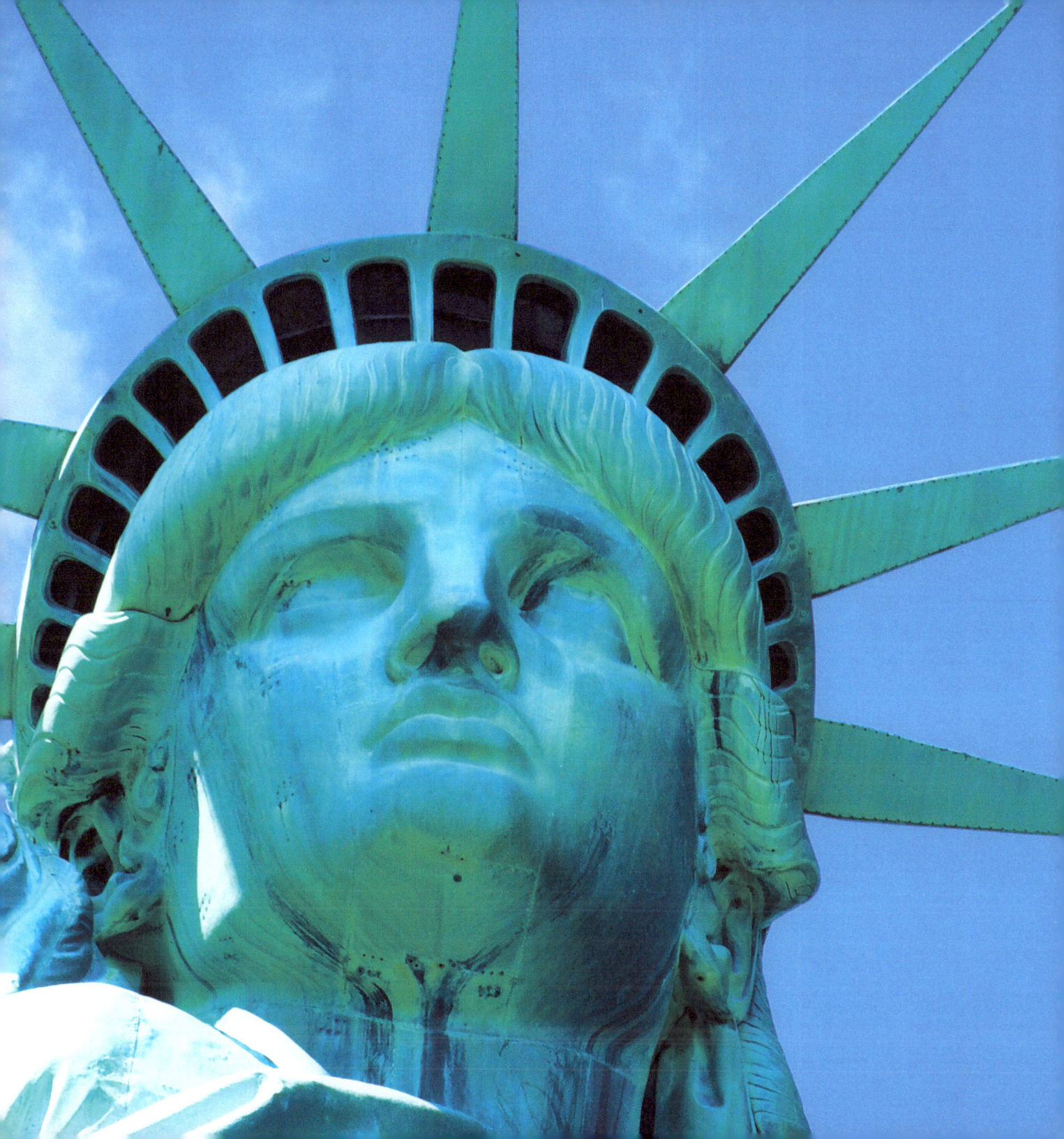

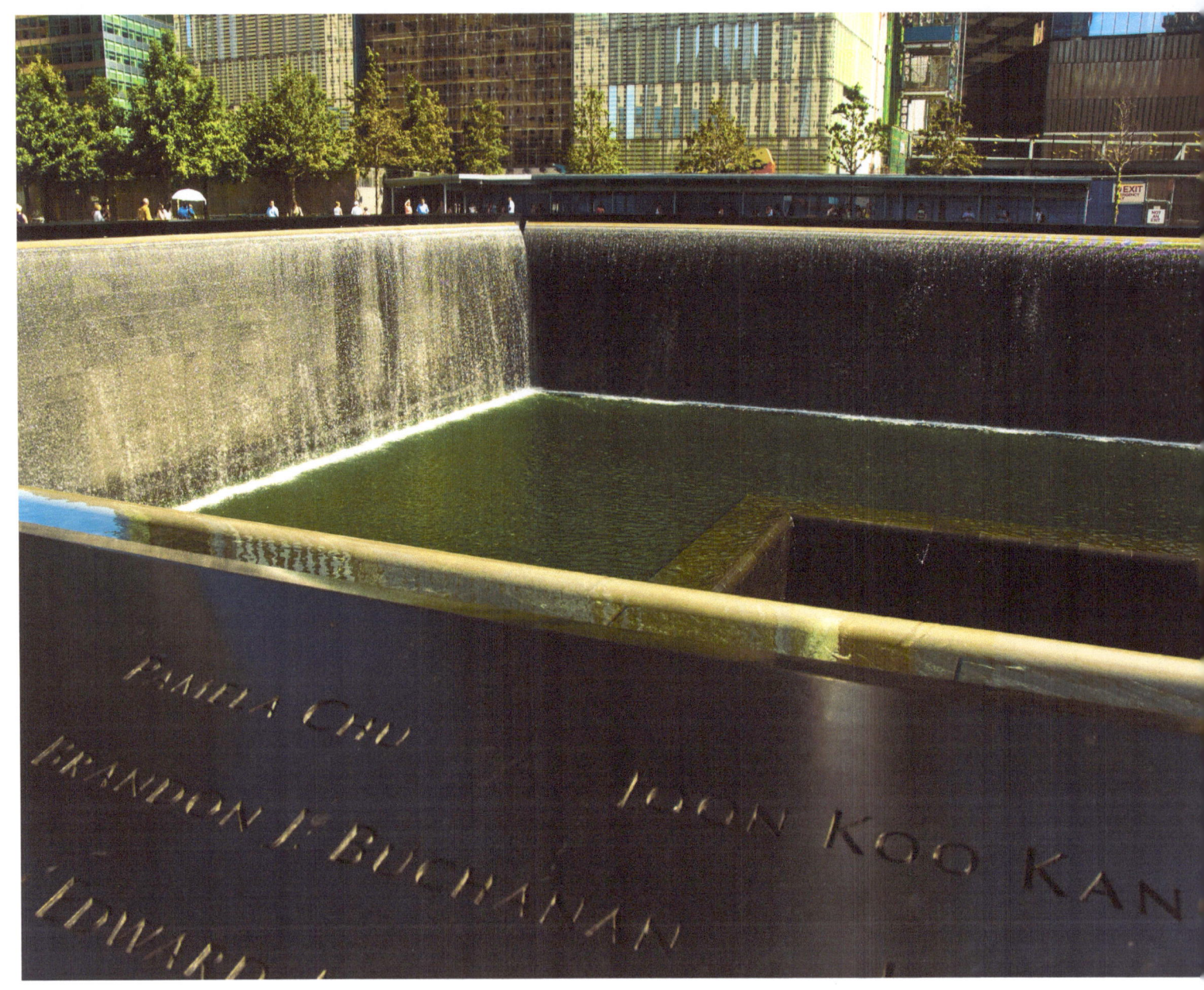

"Two voids that reside in the original footprints."

9/11 MEMORIAL

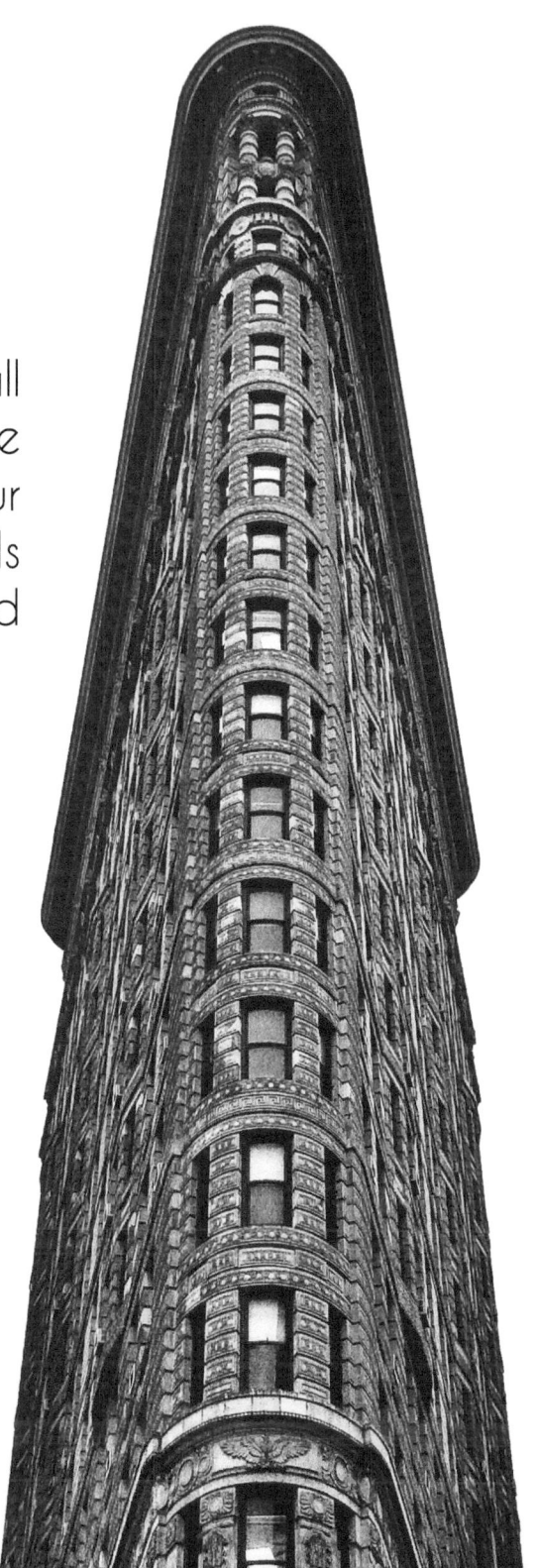

"When your majesty is captivating all of me and I stand before the one who makes my heart adore your majesty beyond what mortal souls could dream and we stand amazed breathless as we come to face."

- Roy, Jason David

FLAT IRON BUILDING

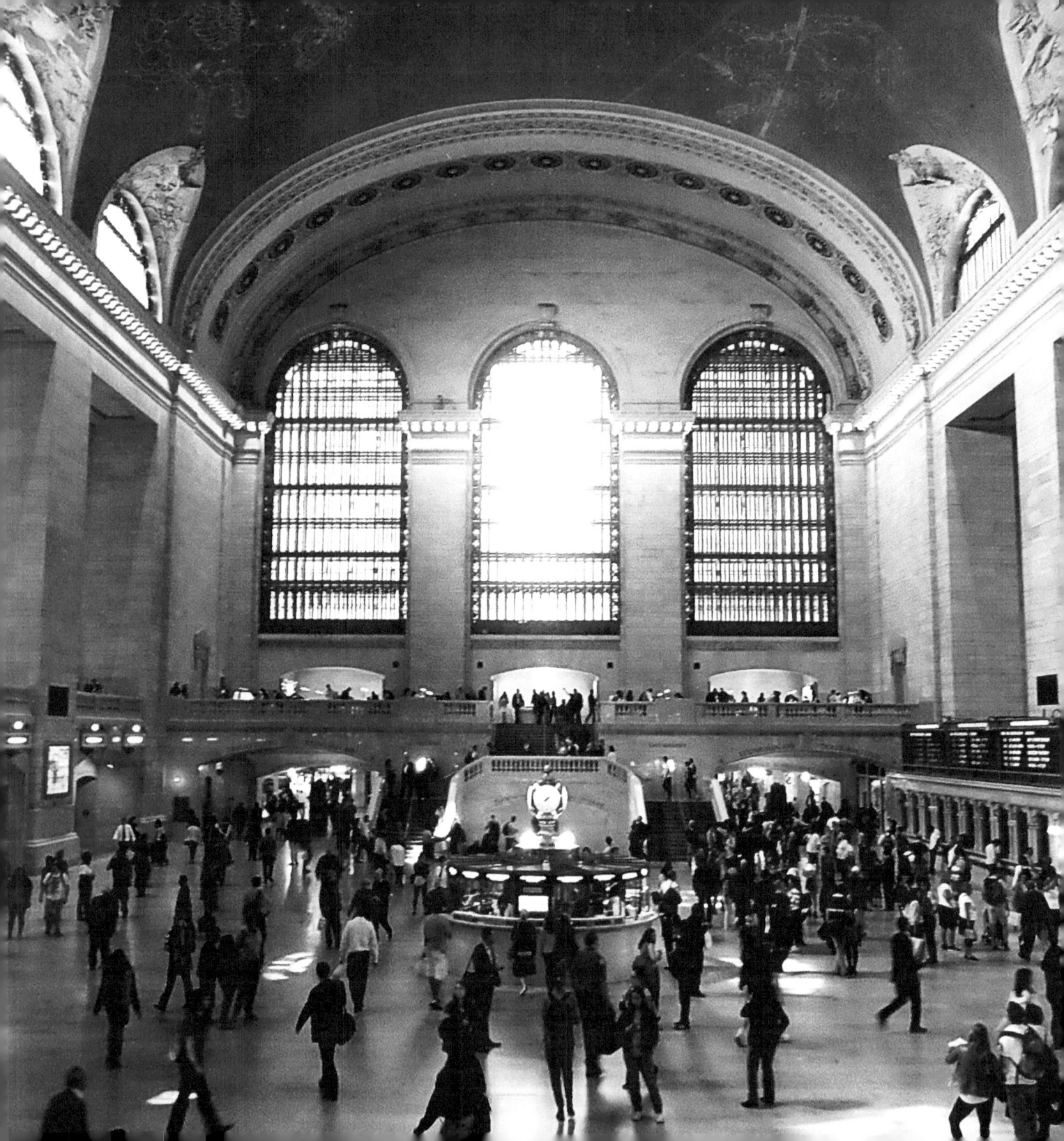

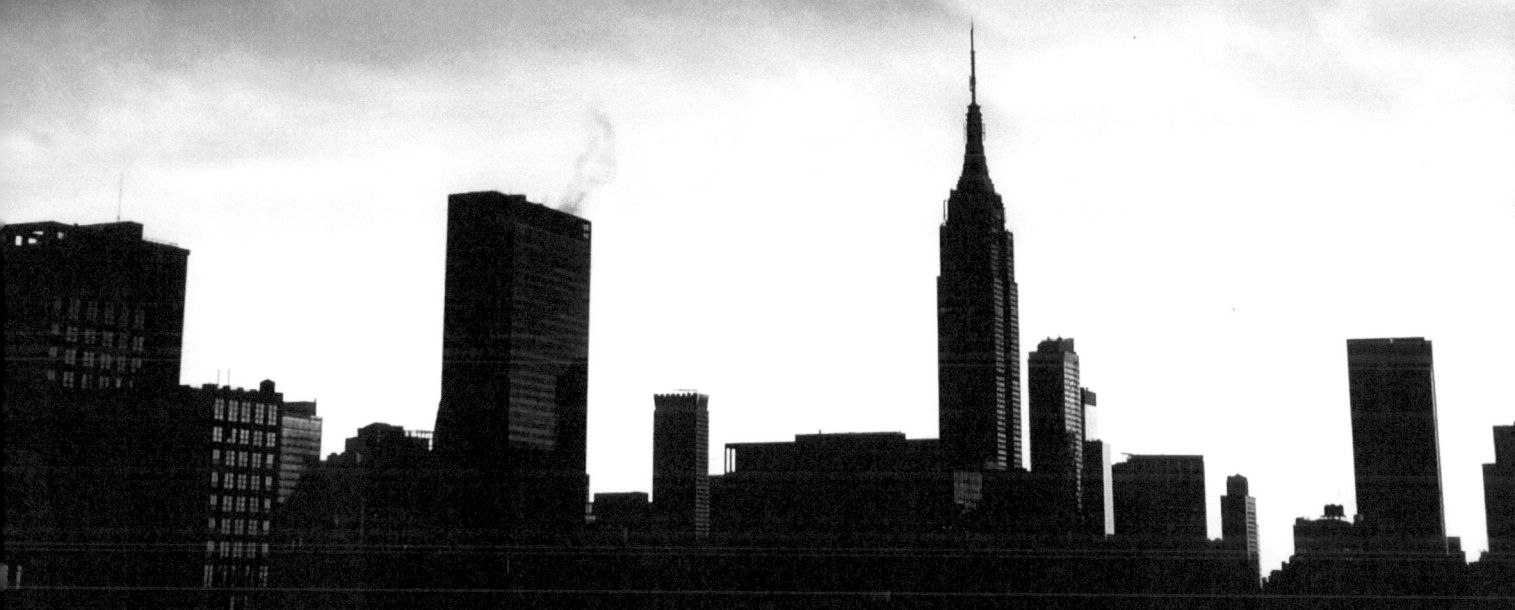

"I get my best ideas in a thunderstorm.
I have the power and majesty of nature on my side."
- Ralph Steadman

Autumn

"If you want to conquer the anxiety of life, live in the moment, live in the breath."

– Amit Ray

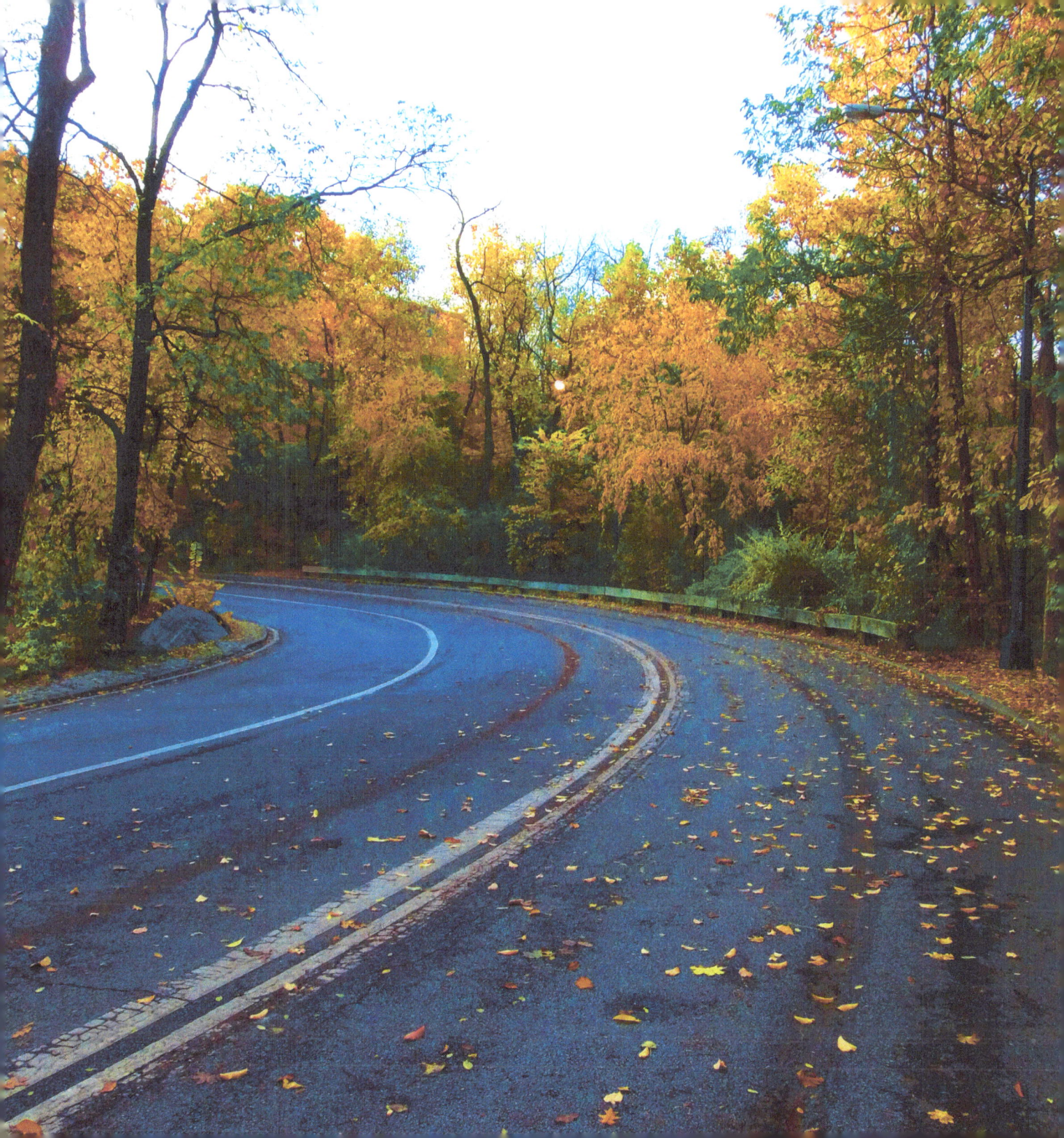

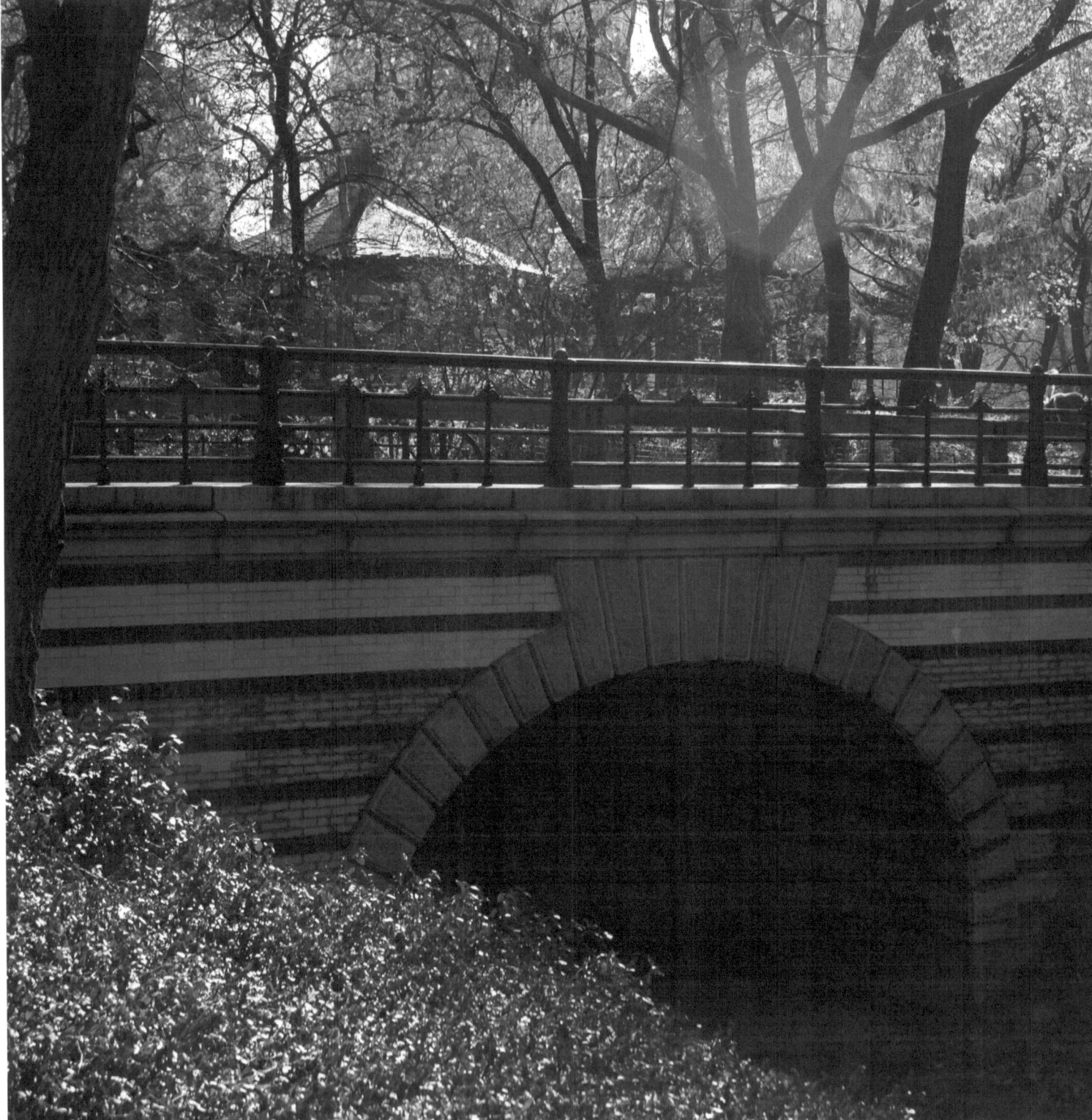

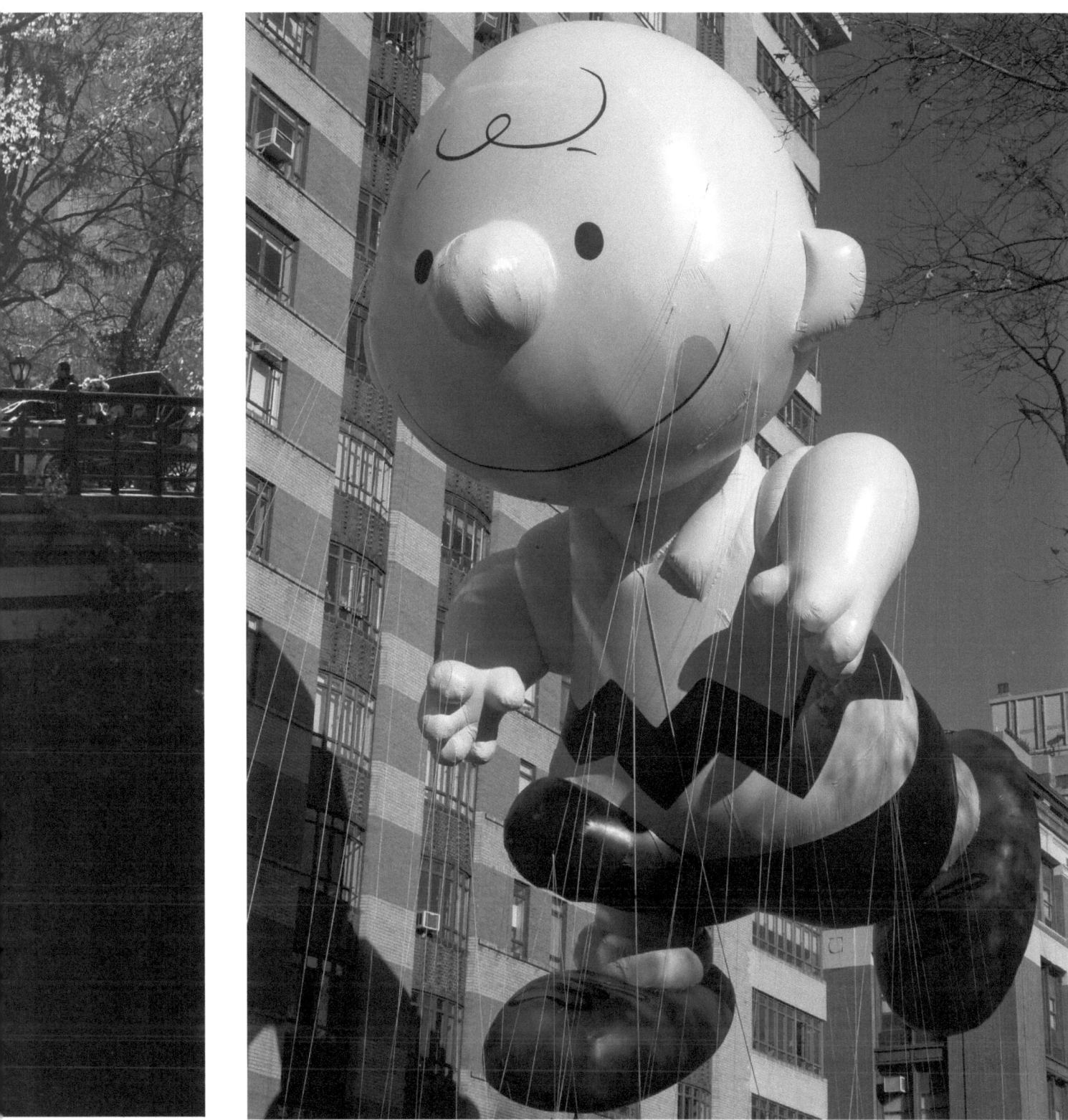

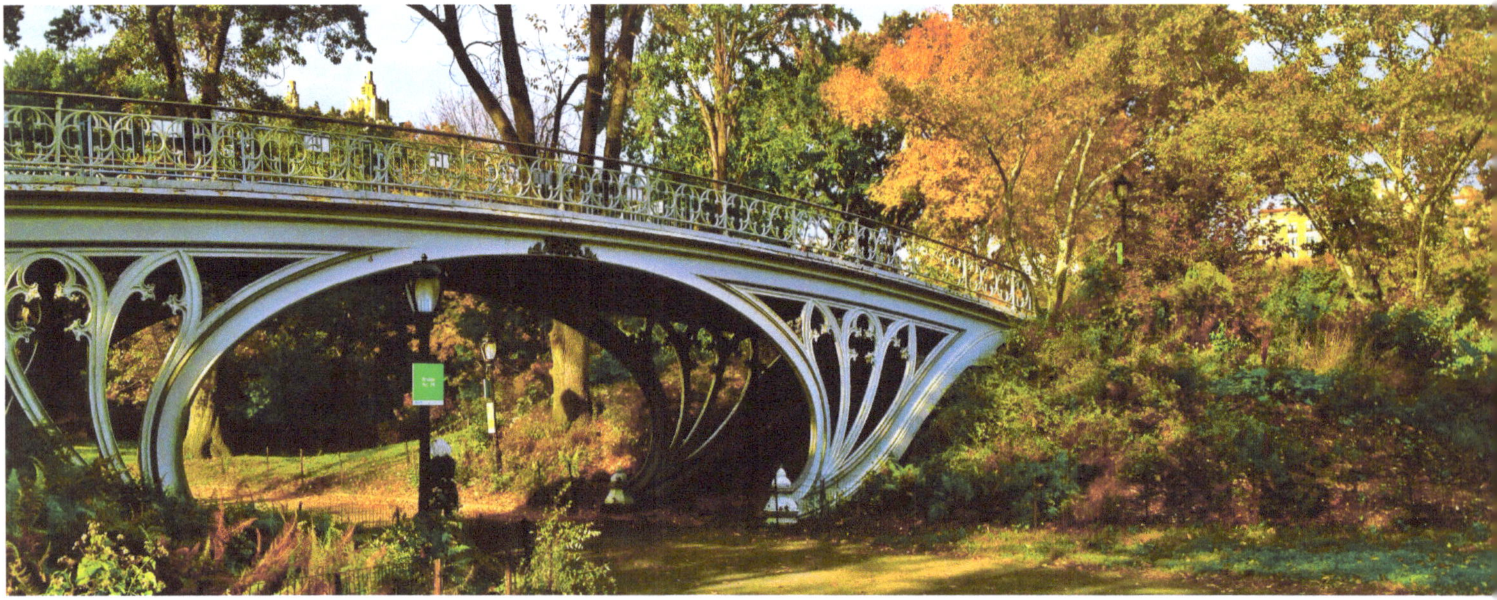

GOTHIC BRIDGE
CENTRAL PARK

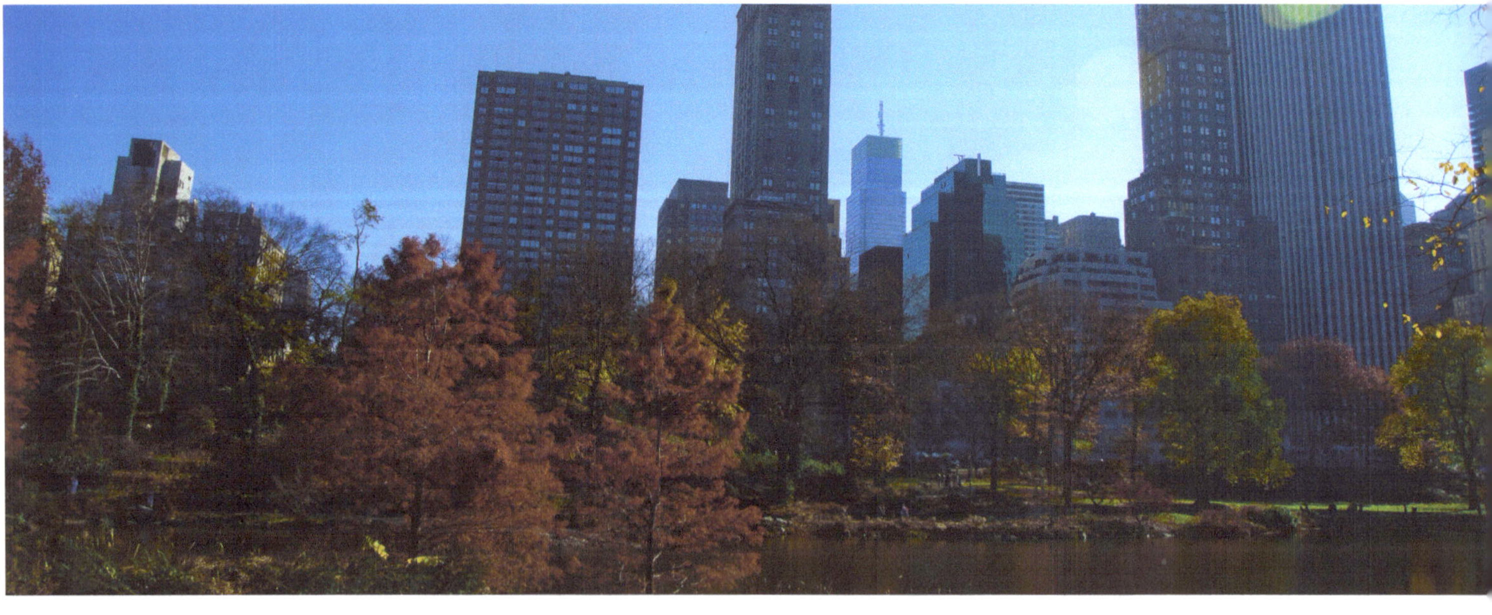

THE POND
CENTRAL PARK

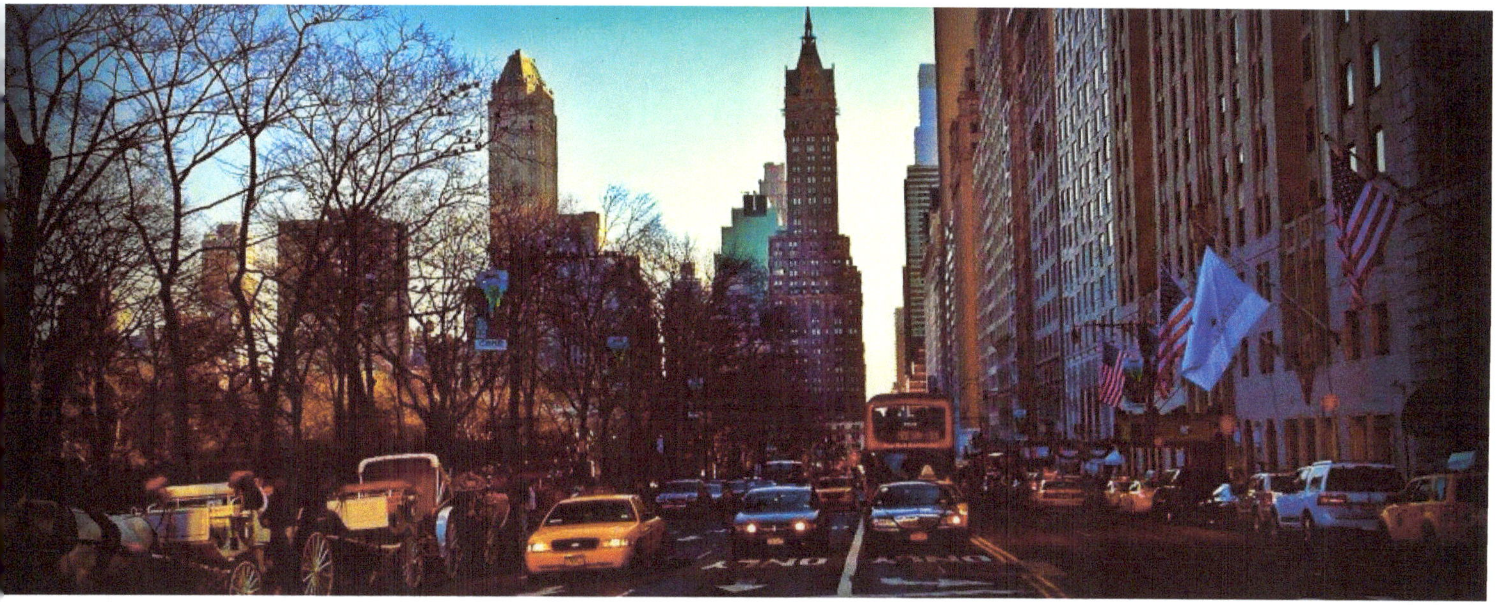

CENTRAL PARK SOUTH

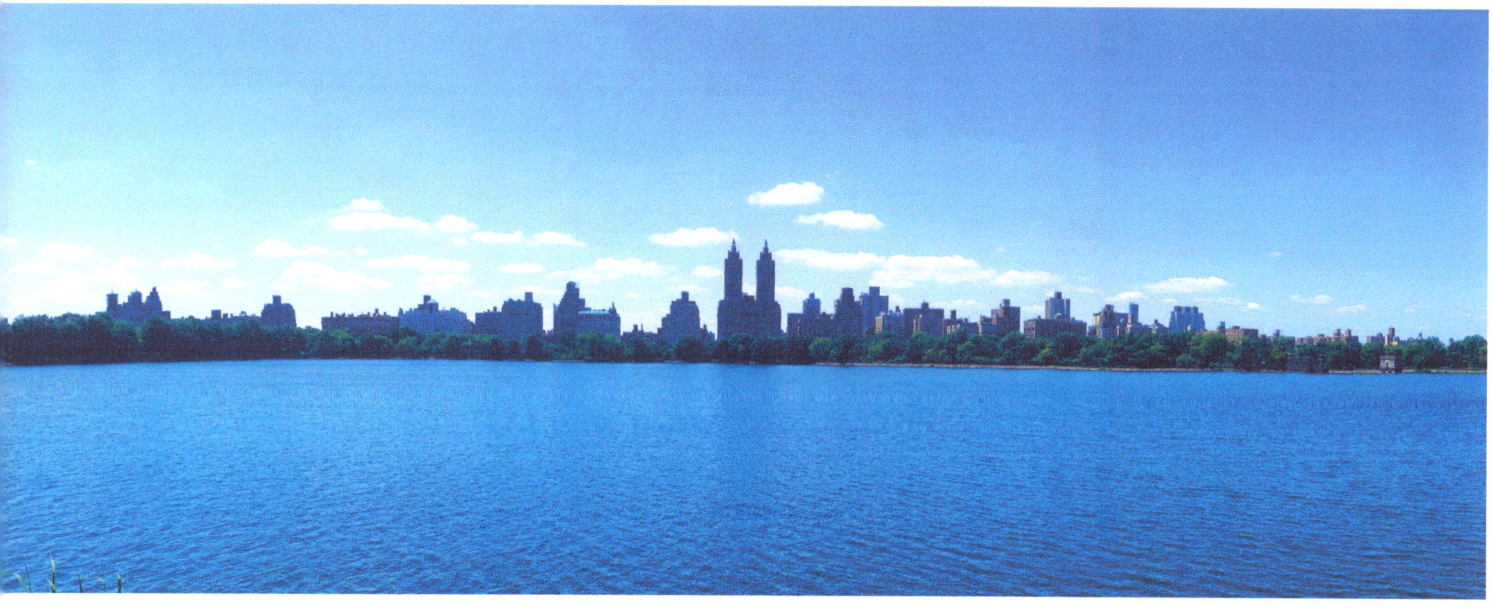

JACQUELINE KENNEDY ONASSIS RESERVOIR
CENTRAL PARK

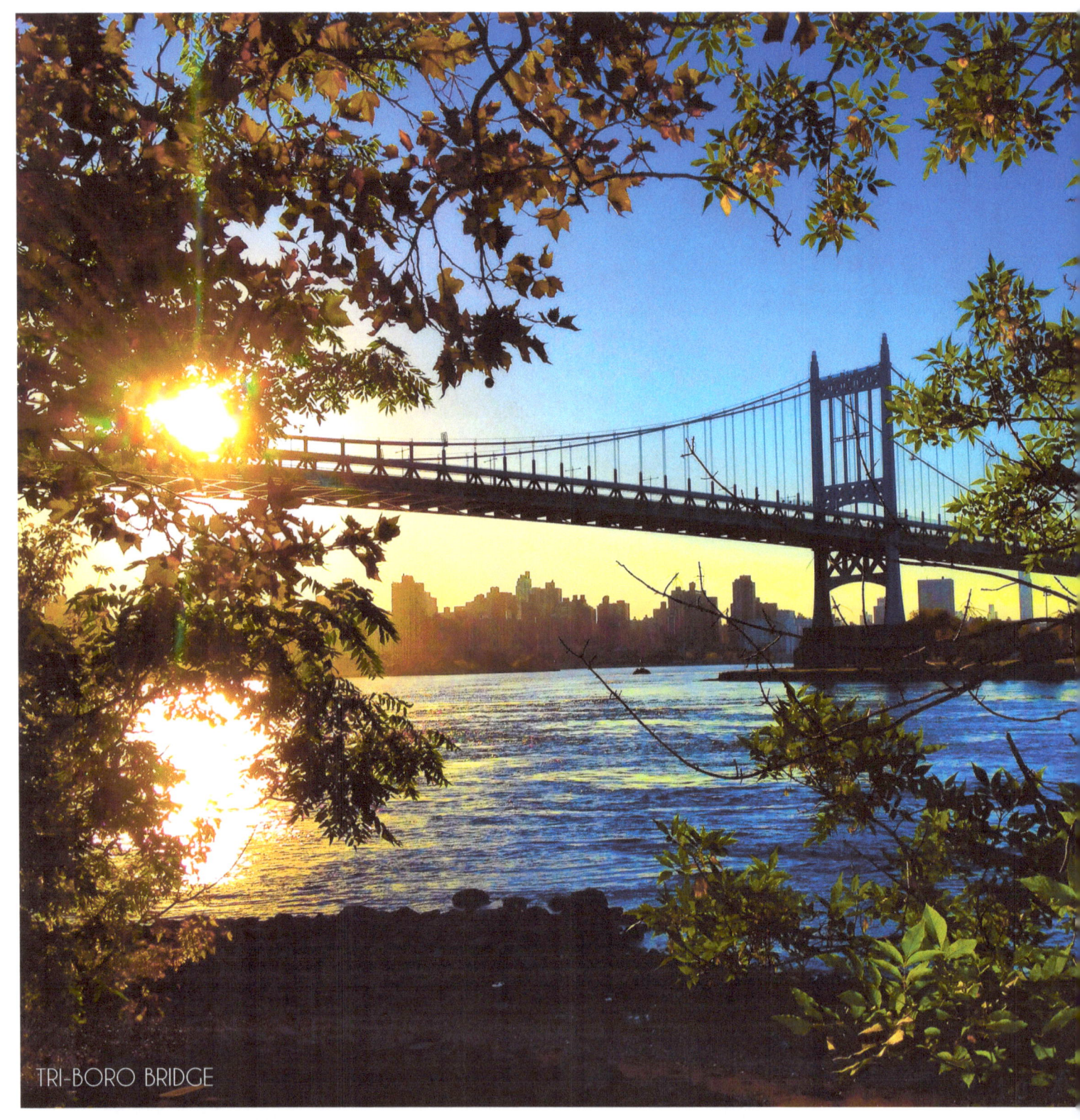

TRI-BORO BRIDGE

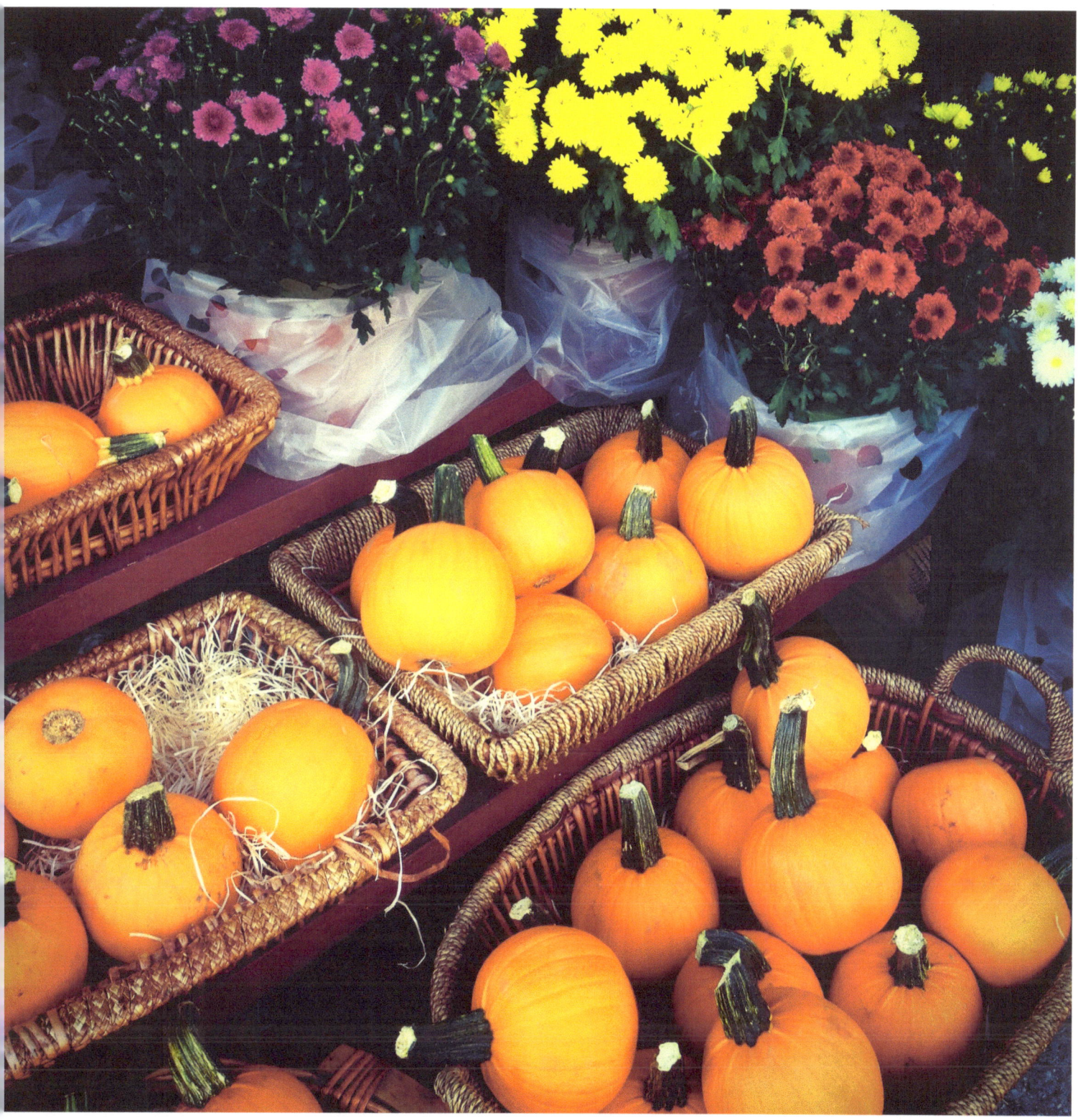

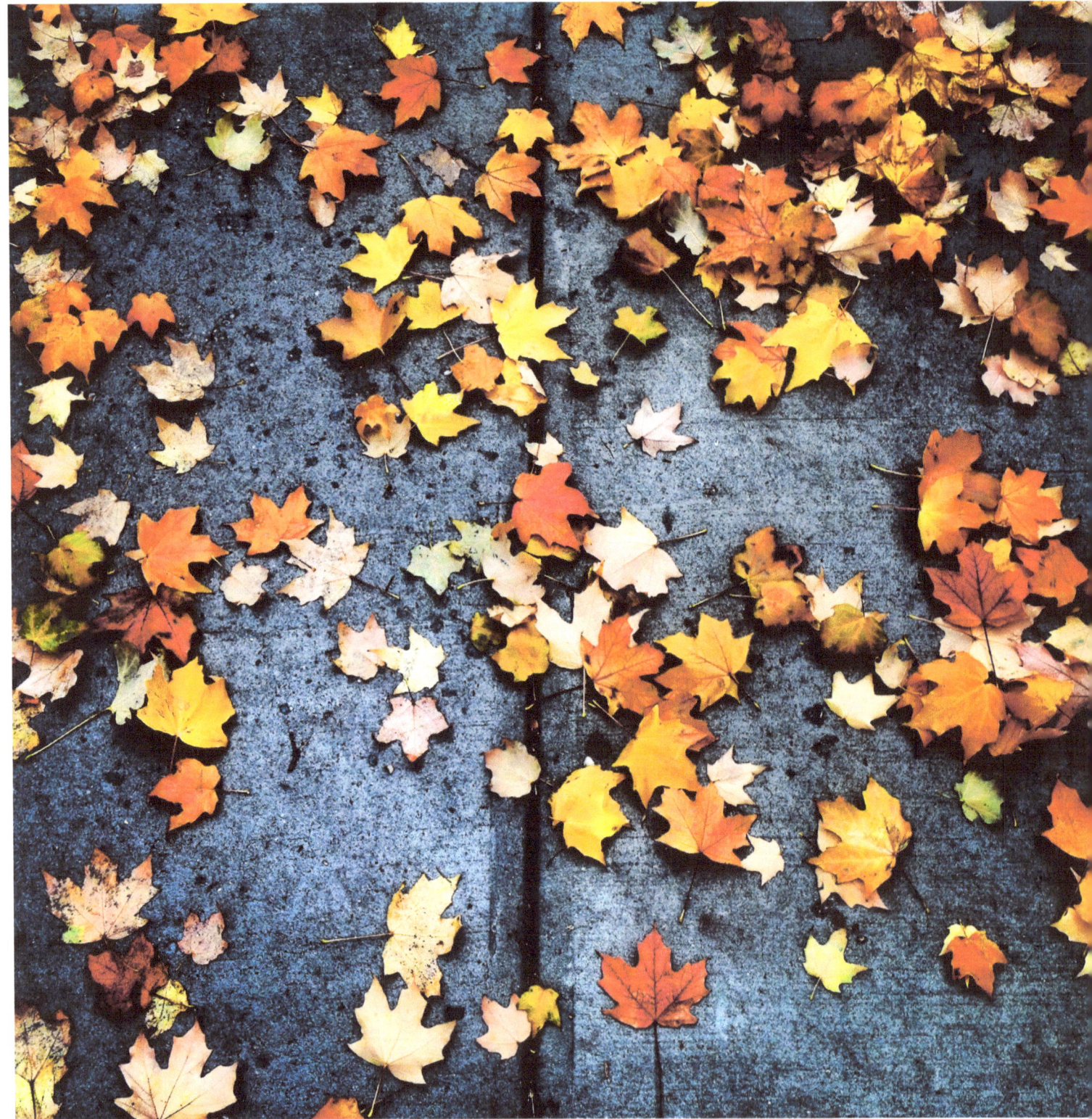

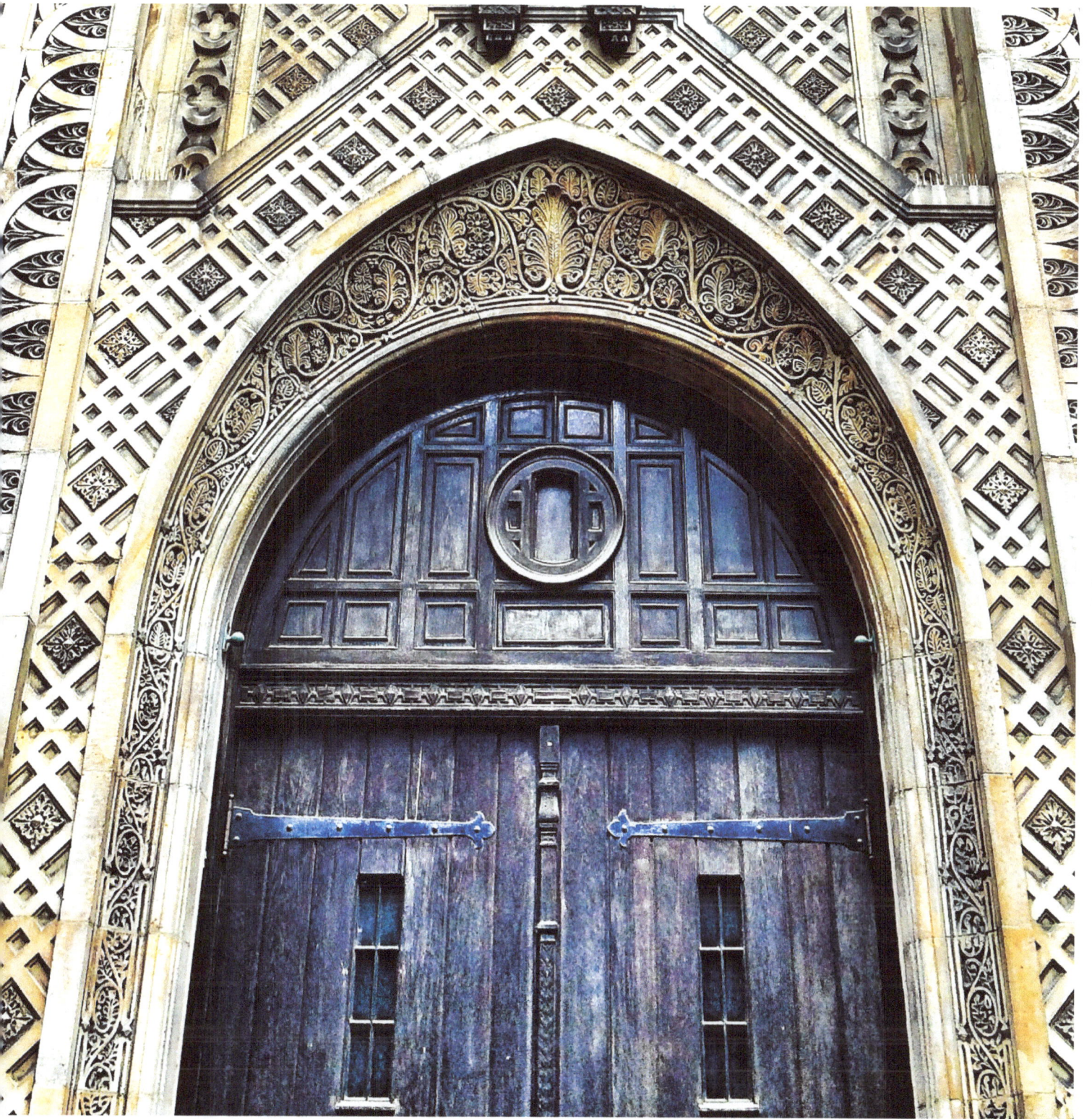

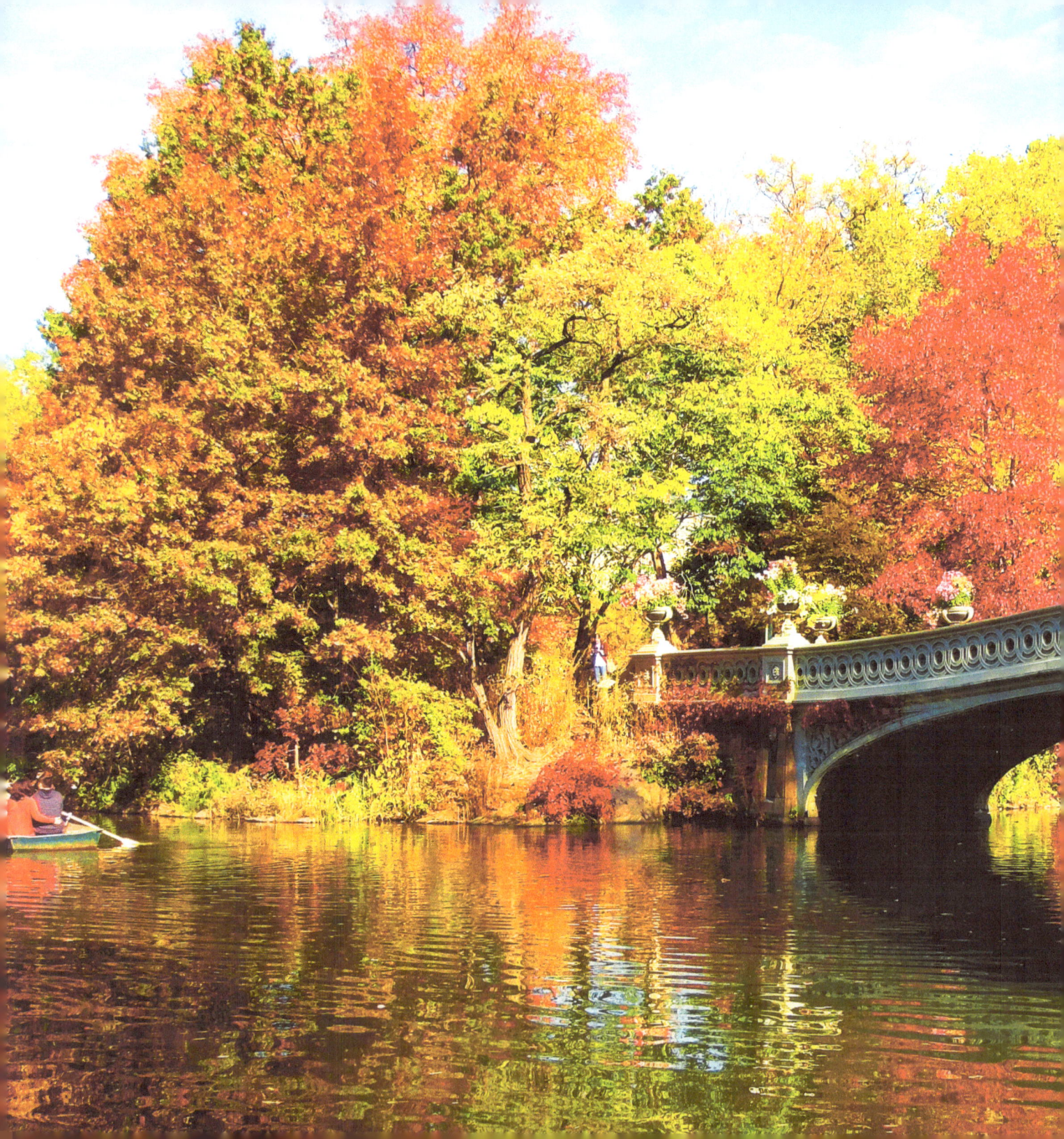

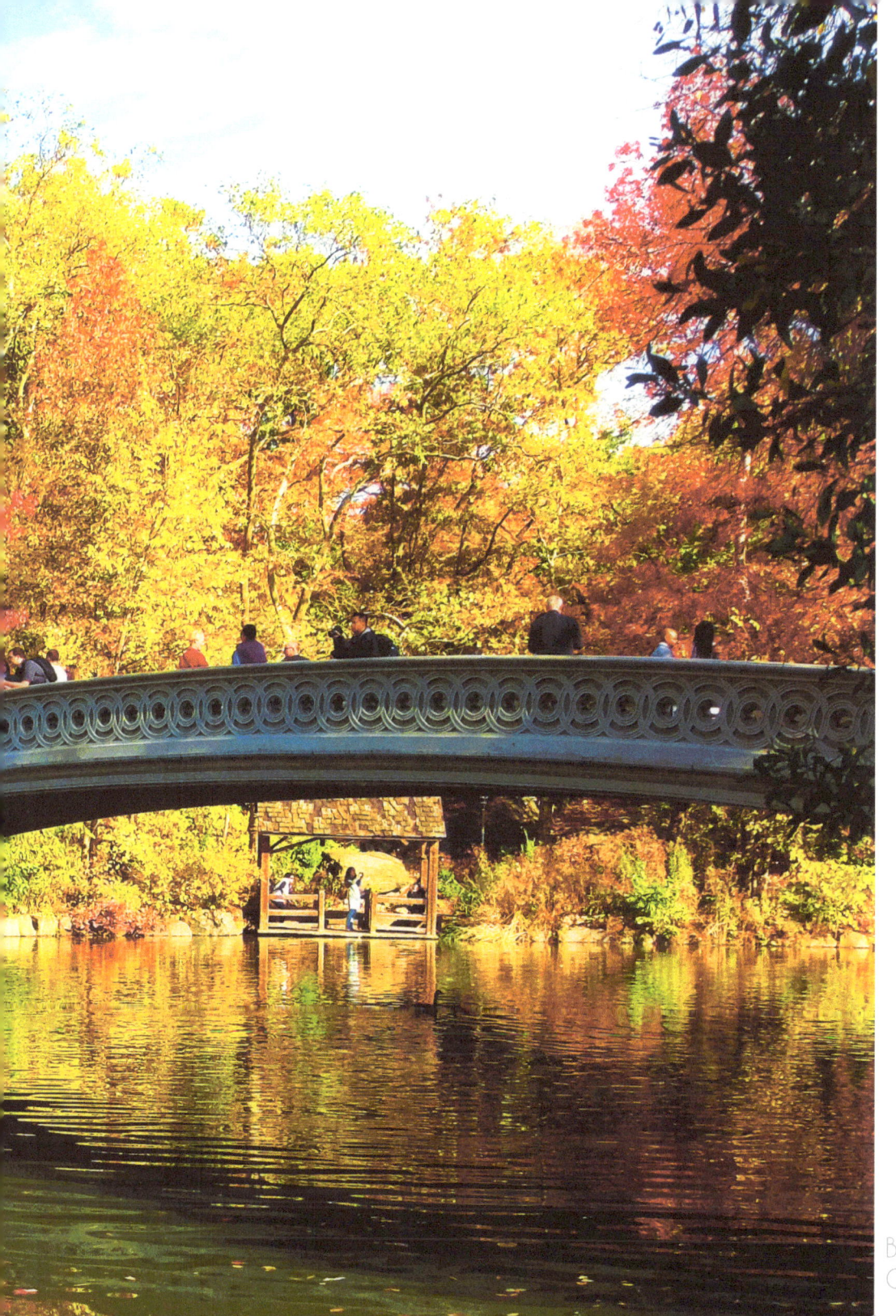

BOW BRIDGE
CENTRAL PARK

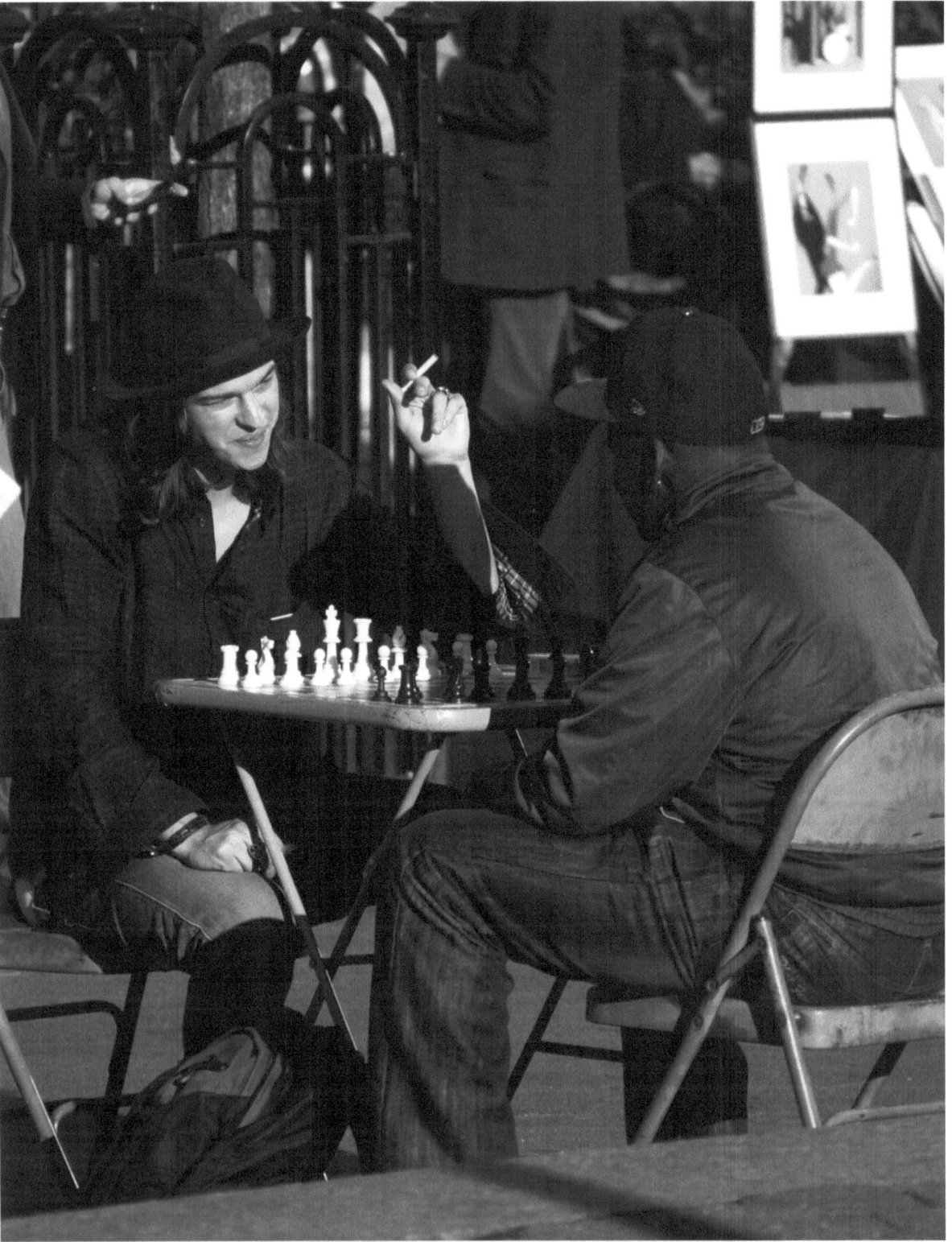

"You must live in the present, launch yourself on every wave, find your eternity in each moment. Fools stand on their island of opportunities and look toward another land. There is no other land; there is no other life but this."

- Henry David Thoreau

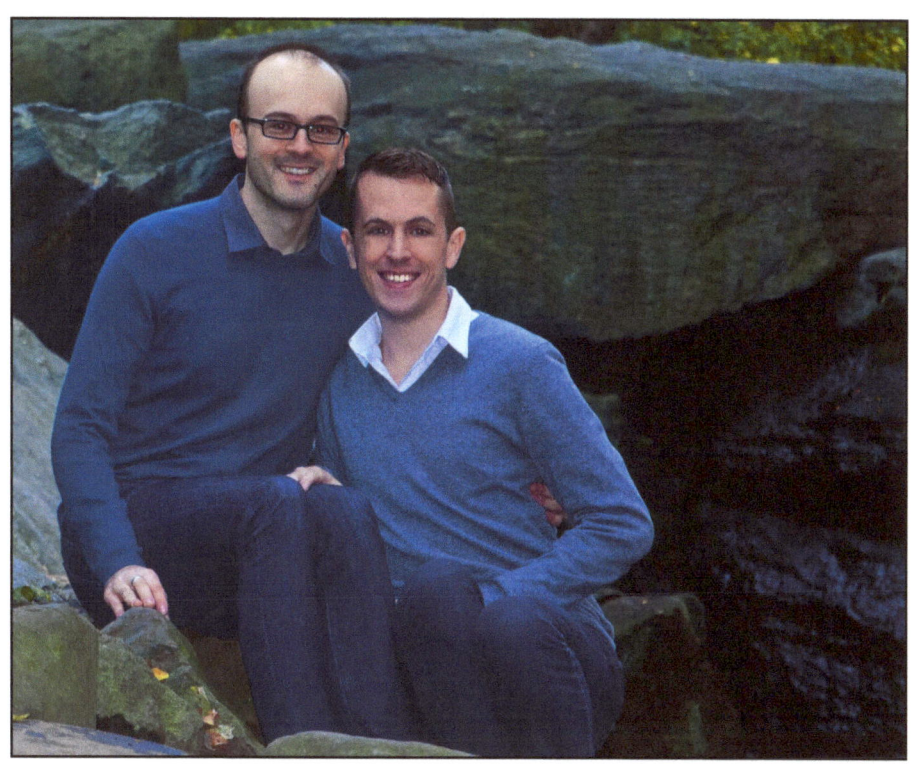

We arrived in New York City at different times, but our love of adventure and beauty took us from our home in Greek Astoria, Queens, to experience everything world's most famous city had to offer. This book tells our two-year story of that experience. We're letting it serve as our testament to the majesty of the city that never sleeps.

Follow Steve: twitter.com/sadams212

Follow Richard: richarddedor.com   twitter.com/richarddedor

Published by Steve Adams & Richard Dedor

ISBN-13: 978-1502906120
ISBN-10: 1502906120

Library of Congress Control Number: 2014918860

Book edited and compiled by Steve Adams & Richard Dedor.

Photo Credits:
Steve Adams: Page 5, 6, 7, 8, 9, 11, 12, 13, 14 (New York Public Library), 16, 17, 18, 19, 20, 21, 22-23, 27, 28 (Upper Right: Subway Sign, Lower Right: Subway Entrance), 29, 30, 31, 33, 35, 36, 37, 39, 42 (Gothic Bridge), 43, 44, 45, 46, 47, 48-49

Richard Dedor: Page 14 (Shake Shack), 15, 25, 26, 28 (Upper Left: Subway Light, Lower Left: Interior Subway), 32, 34, 40, 41, 42 (The Pond), 50

Cover Photo Credits: N (Richard Dedor), Y (Steve Adams), C (Steve Adams)

This title is available for special promotions, premiums, and bulk purchases. For more information, please contact the author at information@richarddedor.com.

Printed in the United States of America

www.ingramcontent.com/pod-product-compliance
Lightning Source LLC
Chambersburg PA
CBHW050810180526

45159CB00004B/1619